MORE PRAISE FOR *NEW RULES FOR WOMEN*

"This book is full of life lessons that all women can get value from. I encourage women to read this book and use these 'new rules' to break the next glass ceiling for other women or to take down the barriers in their own careers."
—Carrie Battaglia, Vice President of Global End User Services,
Hewlett-Packard

"Anne Litwin offers a fascinating discussion of a complex problem. I highly recommend it to all working women who feel that they are falling behind regardless of their hard work."
—Behrooz Fattahi, PhD, 2014 President,
American Institute of Mining, Metallurgical, and Petroleum Engineers,
and 2010 President, Society of Petroleum Engineers International

"I wish I'd had the benefit of Anne's insights when I was first navigating the waters of working relationships. Like many women, I came up through the ranks and bumped up against 'boundary confusion' with friends as my role changed. This book provides valuable and actionable ideas for when and how to deal with these issues!"
—Peggy DePaoli, Director, Hewlett-Packard

"We can all learn a great deal about subtle behavioral patterns and powerful forces that cause women to struggle in work environments. This book offers tools for enhancing morale and creating more supportive professional relationships and dynamics. Anne Litwin demonstrates through her research and case studies that we, men as well as women, have the power to change destructive patterns and transform organizational cultures."
—Joel Seligman, President, University of Rochester

"This book is relevant to both men and women engaged in enterprise work. It offers thought-provoking insights into how women behave differently from men in the workplace and how we can spot, and change, behaviors to make people more productive."
—Lisa Danzer, Solution Executive, Americas Solution Integration and
Design, HP Enterprise Services, and President Emeritus, DFW*ATW

"Anne Litwin has deftly tackled the delicate issue of woman-on-woman aggression. She provides critical insights by documenting and explaining how women's internalized expectations of collaboration and egalitarianism can lead to women damaging each other's careers and provides astute recommendations on how to address the problem."
—*Eve Sprunt, PhD, 2006 President, Society of Petroleum Engineers, and consultant, Eve Sprunt and Associates*

"This book reveals new aspects of women's relationships that I have never seen written about before. It is surprising how women all over the world seem to have the same pattern of interactions that help stop each other from being successful. The situations described in the book are quite familiar to me, and now I see my relations with other women from a different angle."
—*Dr. Barbara Kollenda, Managing Director, ProLubium GmbH*

"Dr. Litwin handles the important and urgent topic of women's relationships and the work environment in a provocative way. Great businesses will work to address this issue, thereby continuing to unleash differentiated talent in their organizations."
—*Susan Arthur, Vice President, Hewlett-Packard*

"Dr. Anne Litwin provides research and insights that help women identify detrimental behaviors and transform them into effective approaches. It is through developing mutually beneficial relationships with men and women that we best advance our organizations, our teams, and our careers."
—*Betty Shanahan, CAE, MBA, Past Executive Director and CEO, Society of Women Engineers*

"This is a brave and important book that will help us leverage our strengths as women and allow us to be a powerful example for men of how to be both friends and productive colleagues in the workplace. Anne's research and case studies sharpened my awareness of woman-to-woman dynamics. This is a good book for a women's study group to read with excellent questions for us to ponder together."
—*Nancy L Seleski, Director, Supply Chain Services & Quality, 3M Industrial Business Group*

New Rules for Women

*Revolutionizing the Way
Women Work Together*

•

Anne Litwin, PhD

THIRD BRIDGE PRESS

Third Bridge Press
839 Bestgate Road, #400
Annapolis, MD 21401
www.thirdbridgepress.com

Quantity sales. Special discounts are available on quantity purchases by corporations, associations, and others. For details, contact the "Special Sales Department" at the address above.

Orders by US trade bookstores and wholesalers. Please contact BCH: (800) 431-1579 or visit www.bookch.com for details.

Publisher's Cataloging-in-Publication
Litwin, Anne H.
  New rules for women : revolutionizing the way women
  work together / Anne Litwin, PhD.
  pages cm
  Includes index.
  LCCN 2014935161
  ISBN 978-0-9820569-8-1 (cl)
  ISBN 978-0-9820569-9-9 (e-book)

  1. Sex role in the work environment. 2. Women
  executives. 3. Women employees. I. Title.

HD6053.L58 2014   331.4
QBI14-600081

Printed in the United States of America

First Edition

18 17 16 15 14   10 9 8 7 6 5 4 3 2 1

Cover design: Kuo Design
Book design and composition: Graffolio
Editing: PeopleSpeak

To my mother, Roslyn Rappaport Litwin,
who taught me about women's friendship

Contents

Preface

Why aren't women more supportive of each other at work? This book helps answer this question, as well as others, and offers a path forward that is good for both women and organizations. It is for any woman who wants to live her dreams and enjoy going to work—because we can do both with the support of other women. It is also for people who want their daughters, sisters, female life partners, and women colleagues and direct reports to do the same. In addition, it is about realizing my own dream of making women's lives better and organizations more productive.

This book is not only for other women and the men they work with—it is also for me. The deeply buried patterns that most of us have learned about relating to other girls and women are mine as well—both the good ones and the bad ones. I learned about the importance of women's friendship and support from my mother's cherished long-term relationships with her women friends. I also experienced her meanness toward me when she felt competitive or threatened and she said and did things to undermine my confidence. I experienced hurtful rejection from girls I thought were my friends in middle and high school who turned on me, betrayed my confidences, and excluded me from social events for reasons that were not obvious to me and usually were never explained. I concluded that the best way to protect myself was to keep my distance from other girls and have only guys for friends. I was a tomboy in early adolescence and preferred having boys for friends as I grew older.

I entered young adulthood with a deep distrust of other women, who I believed would stab me in the back if I let them get too close. At the same time, I stabbed other women in the back by saying things to undermine their credibility or damage their reputations—although I didn't see myself as someone who did that—so I became one of those women who could not be trusted. Fortunately, as a young adult, I participated in the women's movement in the 1970s and gained insights into why these "catty" behaviors happen between women—and I learned to trust other women and become trustworthy myself. (Make no mistake about it, though! I can backslide into old behaviors if I don't stay alert.) I came to realize that each of us, me included, could change, learn to trust each other, and help each other heal from the wounds of the past. I also realized that when we help each other heal, we can turn our focus away from watching our backs with each other and toward doing something together to change the sources of the problem. I began to understand that hurtful behaviors happen for a reason and are not "just the way women are."

This book is for everyone, women and men, who wants to understand and be part of the solution instead of part of the problem. Change always requires examining and becoming aware of our own attitudes and beliefs and then making the choice to change our behaviors to help create trusting relationships. This book is based on the belief that increasing trust and support between women will not only help individual women achieve their dreams but also increase the vitality and success of our organizations.

Why am I focusing on adult women's relationships in the workplace when it is clear that our beliefs and behaviors about girls and women are shaped much earlier in life? Why am I focusing only on women's relationships in the workplace and not on women's and men's relationships with each other at work? Much excellent research and writing have already been done on adolescent girls and boys and on women and men in the workplace.[1] However, not much research has been done on women's relationships with each other at work.

My interest in adult women in the workplace comes from my work as an organization development consultant, leadership development trainer, and executive coach—as well as forty years as a feminist. As a consultant, coach, and trainer for thirty years, I often heard women complaining about feeling betrayed by other women at work. While I also saw many supportive relationships, I saw competent and capable women who, after being promoted, were undermined or driven out by their female colleagues. I heard complaints about female bosses being tougher on women subordinates than on men and about hurt feelings and resentments between women colleagues that created barriers to their work relationships years after the offending incident. Such negative dynamics can seriously damage women's careers, and I wanted to find a way to change them. I decided to focus on this topic for my doctoral dissertation, completed in 2008, and I have continued to expand on this research and apply the findings to my consulting practice (see the appendix for a description of the research design).

As a feminist I am committed to making women's lives better, and this is also my life purpose. Healthy organizations and the success of adult women are my areas of expertise and my passions. Working with adolescent girls and boys to help them grow into healthy adults continues to be important for others to do.[2] I believe that adult women have an unprecedented opportunity to make a change at this moment in our country when 51 percent of all managerial and professional jobs are held by women and 71 percent of US women with children under eighteen earn a paycheck,[3] yet only 3 percent of Fortune 500 CEOs are women and women's pay still averages only 75 cents on the dollar for the same work as men.[4] Of course, not every woman wants to, could, or will become a CEO, but companies with the highest number of women in top management do show a 35 percent higher return on investment (ROI) than comparable companies, so it is in the interest of organizations to ensure that women advance.[5] Organizations also need to understand how company policies, procedures, and norms encourage or discourage women's relationships and advancement.

One goal in this book is, then, to help women realize their dreams. Another is to increase the vitality and success of organizations. I believe that both can be accomplished when women, with support from male colleagues and bosses, can develop more supportive relationships with one another and work together to change their workplaces to be more productive for all.

Acknowledgments

Conducting this research and writing this book represent important milestones in my lifelong quest to improve the lives of women—my passion for forty years. I hoped to uncover something through the research process that would help women in organizations understand what is happening when they don't feel supported by other women and how to change those dynamics—and I have been able to do that. The hardest part about collecting the data for this research was to stop collecting data. It was difficult to feel satisfied that I had included enough women's voices. My good friends were finally able to persuade me to stop collecting data so that I could write this book and share my findings—and make a difference. But I will really never be finished with this research and will probably keep expanding it for the rest of my life through involving women in this conversation about our relationships in the workplace.

It was, of course, daunting to contemplate writing a book. The problem wasn't that I didn't have enough to say but that I had too much to say from the voluminous amount of research data and all the case studies from my consulting practice and my life. However, I have been giving speeches about the findings from this research for some time now, and my audiences made it clear what they needed to know and were most interested in. Their feedback helped me focus and choose which of the data to keep and which to put aside.

I am grateful for all the support and encouragement I got along the way. Both the research and this book are accomplishments that would not have been possible without the love and support of many people. First, I want to acknowledge the generous daily support of my life partner, Michael Willard. Your encouragement to stay focused on this massive project made it possible for me to finish it.

Next, I want to thank Matthews Hamabata, my academic mentor and dissertation chair, along with committee members David Rehorick, Judy Stevens Long, Rianna Moore, and Lynn O'Brien Hallstein. Thank you for your constant encouragement and belief in me, especially when I was unsure of my way. Your steady guidance and expertise were so helpful, especially when my passion for my subject tended to sometimes blind me to my data.

I want to thank my sister, Jane Litwin Lyss, and my mother, Roslyn Litwin, for their encouragement and patience with me while I juggled work, school, research, and writing—sometimes instead of spending time with them. While my mother did not live to see the book finished, I know she is proud of me.

I am blessed with a wonderful circle of friends who have been there for me all the way through my doctorate and book-writing journeys, including Mary Lou Michael, Donna Healey, Jane Critchlow, Jen Cohen, Nanci Burk, Teressa Moore Griffin, Tom Finn, and Bill Woodson. Many other women in my circle of friends were also encouraging and patient when I had to disappear for stretches of time to focus on my work and helped me celebrate my accomplishments. They include Marcia Goffin, Marsha Clark, Marcia Hyatt, Narandja Milanovich, Karen Oshry, Judith Leibowitz, Sharon Bueno Washington, Martha Comfort, Karen Young, Jeanette Millard, Jean and Kiyoko Fujiu, and the women of Maude's—Marilyn Bronzi, Nancy Brown-Jamison, Joanne Carr, Lucia Edmonds, Adrienne Lee, Mary Lou Michael, and Emily Cuby Eberhardt Vincent. I also thank Rene Minvielle for her patient work with the technical aspects of producing this document.

A special thanks to my wonderful and patient editor, Sharon Goldinger.

Last, but not least, I want to thank the 119 women who generously gave their time to participate in my study. You were truly my coresearchers, and I hope you feel that you made a contribution to improving women's lives through your participation.

Introduction

Behind the curtain of sisterhood lies a myriad of
emotional tangles that can wreak havoc in women's
relationships with each other.
—LUISE EICHENBAUM AND SUSIE ORBACH, *Between Women*

This book seeks to answer a range of questions about the emotional tangles that can wreak havoc on women's relationship dynamics in the workplace:

- Why don't women support each other more at work?
- Why do women so often feel betrayed by other women at work?
- Why does sabotage happen so frequently between women at work?
- Why do so many women say they prefer working for a man?
- Can gossip be positive?
- What are friendship rules and what have they got to do with the workplace?
- What about cultural differences?

This book will provide some answers to these questions, as well as stimulate you to become more aware of your own attitudes and behaviors. It also offers tips and strategies that can help change your relationships with women colleagues and change your work environment.

This book is different from popular books on women being mean to each other at work. First of all, it is based on my original research. It was not written to shock anyone. It was written with a lot of caution and concern about not wanting to validate or perpetuate negative stereotypes about women being catty and backstabbing. We need to understand what is going on when women aren't supportive and feel betrayed. And happily, most of the time women are supportive. But when we aren't, we need to be more honest with ourselves about what part we each play and what kind of role model we are for girls and women. We need to be conscious of the ways our workplace environments set us up against each other and what could be done to change these workplace cultures. We cannot come together to make these changes if we do not trust each other and see the causes of our behaviors only as personality problems that some people have or as "just the way women are."

Women's Friendships

Why a book on women's friendships at work when common wisdom says that friendships do not belong in the workplace? "After all," people often say, "the workplace is for working. Talking about personal and social matters does not belong and wastes time that should be used for real work." First, it is unrealistic to think that we don't need to have good relationships at work. We need good relationships with others to get the help and information we need, to establish good teamwork, to foster good communication with coworkers, and to develop in our jobs. We also need good relationships to have the type of work environments that validate us and motivate us to do our best. And second, for many women, between the demands of work and the demands of family life, we do not have time left over to get our social needs met outside of work.[1] Women friends have always been important as a source of strength to manage our increasingly complex world.[2]

We do sometimes form important friendships at work. The health of these relationships has triple importance for our sense of well-being and our satisfaction with both our work and outside lives. Because our relationships with other women at work are a source of psychological health, growth, and empowerment, especially for women working in male-dominated environments and professions, we need to find pathways to invest in strengthening those relationships.[3]

While much has been written about what's positive about women's relationships, there has been an absence of research on the shadow side—the patterns of relationship that are not positive between women at work. This absence may be the result of an overreaction in the attempt to correct for the negative stereotypes that have made it almost taboo to talk about anything negative in women's relationships, especially in the context of the workplace. Such concerns are well founded, but we must acknowledge what isn't always positive so that we can find the pathway to change those negative dynamics. This book will help light the way down this less-explored path.

What Is in This Book and How to Use It

This book is organized to inform you about important research findings from an expansion of my doctoral dissertation and case studies from my consulting practice. The expanded research included women in the United States, Spain, China, Mexico, and India who participated in group sessions and in-depth interviews. The participants were from a wide range of work environments (for example, technology, financial services, healthcare, government, academia, nonprofits). More details about the research design can be found in the appendix. Each chapter provides exercises to help you gain awareness and skills along with strategies to make changes in yourself and your organization. The book is designed to open your eyes, validate what you may already know, and suggest pathways for different possibilities for women in organizations.

One of the many surprises from this study was the emergence of something I'm calling "friendship rules," which have turned out to be of great interest to the audiences with whom I have been talking. Understanding these rules is central to understanding why certain patterns of relationship between women occur at work. For that reason, chapter 1 explains what friendship rules are, how they operate in the context of the workplace, and how they can combine with organizational culture to contribute to misunderstandings between women coworkers. Examples from a diverse group of study participants, located both in the United States and in India, China, Spain, and Mexico in a wide variety of organizations, help the concepts come to life.

Many women report that they expect something different from women bosses than they expect from bosses who are men. Chapters 2 and 3 explore the different expectations that women have of women bosses and the difficulties this can create. In these chapters, we will also consider why women often say they prefer working for a man and examine some double binds for women bosses who have a masculine style. We will explore the implications of having fluid boundaries as sources of both support and confusion, and we will consider how workplace cultures make it difficult for women to be supportive of each other. We will also explore strategies for overcoming these challenges.

Gossip is a common pattern of behavior in the workplace, and chapter 4 considers some positive sides of gossip. Both women and men gossip at work, although women seem to be judged more harshly for doing it and get tagged as "catty," a term not generally applied to men for the same behavior. One of the surprises from my study is the positive role that gossip can play and the need for new language to explain it. I introduce a new term, "transknitting," and consider when gossip is constructive and when it's not. We will also consider tools that individuals and managers can use to repair relationships when they are damaged.[4]

Popular culture portrays women's workplace relationships as largely negative, and women in my audiences have been eager to share stories of sabotage between women at work with the hope of finding solutions.[5] Chapter 5 describes a continuum of intentionally hurtful behaviors. These behaviors range from excluding a coworker from social interactions to intentional efforts to damage a coworker's career. We will explain why these behaviors happen and the ways societal and workplace cultures help produce them, along with solutions.

In chapter 6, we will consider some reasons why the women in this study felt they could not do anything to change some common behaviors they experience with other women. We will consider the implications of what many study participants said was "just the way women are" and explore what else could be true. We will also suggest strategies at the organizational and interpersonal levels for preventing and stopping negative behaviors.

No discussion of women in the workplace would be complete without acknowledging the ways in which women are different. So in chapter 7, we will review some important ways that gender, race, ethnicity, and sexual orientation, along with other differences, interact to result in differences in how we experience organizations. We will also discuss how we can, and need to, acknowledge our differences before we can work together to discover our mutual interests.

In the final chapter, chapter 8, we consider six case studies where some of the practices discussed in this book have been applied. We also offer individual coaching tips and some organizational change strategies.

The focus of this book is on how women's friendship culture can add value to an organization and enhance morale and productivity among work groups. By developing awareness, skills, and a positive shared vision, we can shift the negative dynamics between us, join forces to change organizational cultures, and reclaim and cultivate positive relational dynamics with other women in the workplace.

1

The Context:
Friendship Rules in a "Man's World"

Who does she think she is? I thought she was my friend!

One day, during a routine coaching session, a female client who is a sales rep complained bitterly about an experience she had just had with a woman customer. She was deeply hurt and upset and felt personally betrayed. She explained that her customer, someone she had worked with for a long time, had decided to change vendors and was no longer employing her company—or her. And the worst part of it was that my client found out about the change from someone else—not from her customer. When she told me the story and said, "Who does she think she is? I thought she was my friend," she also said, "I would have expected this from a man but not from a woman!" I thought, "Really? She's a customer. Doesn't this happen in business all the time?" I wondered where this expectation of personal loyalty from women, but not from men, came from. Then I realized that this sense of disappointment and personal betrayal in the workplace context was familiar—that I had heard versions of this disappointment from my women clients many times before. I got curious about where these expectations were coming from and how the workplace context might contribute to the experience of disappointment—and the seeds of my research were sown.

What my research found is that women carry their egalitarian friendship rules, or relational expectations (also known as "relational images"), into the workplace, where they clash with the hierarchical norms that dominate most workplace cultures.[1] This clash sets us up to be disappointed by each other in ways that can feel personal and can damage our relationships. This finding gives us an angle on understanding the source and causes of women's disappointment with each other. It provides a lens that opens up a new way of seeing women's relational dynamics at work and sheds light on a new pathway to understanding and change.

Let's be clear—for the purpose of gaining awareness about some important patterns of behavior that can help us see ways to change, we will be making generalizations about women and about men—and these generalizations will not always be true for every woman or every man who is reading this book. Just notice where these generalizations may or may not resonate with your experience and keep an open mind about these patterns of behavior for others. Now let's unpack these ideas. What are friendship rules, and what do we mean by "friendship rules in a 'man's world'"?

What Are Friendship Rules?

We begin to develop friendship rules at a very young age. By the time my step-granddaughter was four, she was talking about the rules for being a friend. She was learning that if you did this kind of thing, you would make a friend, and if you did that kind of thing, you could lose a friend. In middle school, girls ages nine to thirteen are even more focused on "who is my friend, who is not my friend, what do I have to do to get invited to the party, or what did I do to not get invited?" Excellent research on adolescent girls also shows that by the time girls get to high school, they are less focused on figuring out what the rules are for being friends with girls and more focused on getting the attention of boys—the friendship rules they have learned earlier are still there, but they are receding from their consciousness.[2]

By the time we are adults, our friendship rules have become embedded as a set of filters, but for the most part, we are no longer conscious of them. The problem comes when we enter the workplace, carrying with us everything we have learned, including this set of filters. We react to each other and interpret the behavior of other women through that set of filters and we don't even know we are doing it.

Both women and men have friendship rules, or expectations, but they are different because of gender socialization.[3] Even though the world is changing all the time, the societal messages to girls and boys through the media and role models still differ from each other in terms of what behaviors are expected for girls and boys. Boys learn through games about winning and losing, being more conscious of status, and being more transactional. For example, if I don't choose you for my team, it is just a transaction and not about whether I like you or not. In contrast, even though girls are more involved in sports than in the past, girls' games are still teaching about getting along and about being nurturing. In girls' games, relationships matter more than winning or losing.

Workplace stories are still commonly told that men can have a vehement disagreement at a team meeting and then go out for a beer after work because the disagreement is just a win-lose kind of thing and not about the relationship. But when women disagree at work, it can mean the end of the relationship forever. For women, disagreement can feel personal, and they don't know how to recover from that. Men can just walk out of the workplace and have a beer together because their friendship rules are different and provide filters for interpreting workplace interactions in a way that is not personal.

The participants in my study confirmed what scholars have found about women's friendship expectations: there is a core set of rules or expectations.[4] Table 1 shows that these expectations include unswerving loyalty, trustworthiness, and the ability to keep confidences. Friends share gossip and air problems, are good listeners, offer self-disclosure, practice equality and unconditional acceptance, affirmation, sympathy,

TABLE 1. Common friendship rules for adult women

Show unswerving loyalty and trustworthiness.

Give unconditional acceptance while seldom disapproving.

Keep confidences.

Share gossip and air problems.

Be a good listener.

Self-disclose.

Practice equality.

Don't discuss friendship rules.

and healing—and they do not discuss or negotiate their friendship rules or expectations.

Cultural differences and other factors make it unlikely that all women share the exact same friendship expectations. However, the taboo against discussion means that mismatched assumptions may not be discovered until damage has been done to a relationship, a problem we will focus on later. But for now, let's get clearer about how the context of the workplace makes a difference.

Friendship Rules in a "Man's World"

Men's friendship rules, which emphasize activity and status, fit more neatly within the norms of the hierarchical workplace, and this is where the problem lies for women's relationships. Women's friendship rules are often at odds with workplace norms and can create confusion between women colleagues about what to expect from each other in the workplace environment.[5] In fact, it is not just that men's friendship rules fit more neatly within workplace norms, it is that most workplace cultures were actually set up by men because they were there first.[6] Workplace norms, or cultures, typically reflect and reward masculine values such as being task focused and hierarchical with an expectation of winning and losing. Women's friendship rules are more egalitarian. Let's take a look at how these rules can clash with workplace norms through a story from the research.

Alice, an Asian American engineer in her fifties, told the story of a woman coworker who was a very good friend and how their relationship did not survive:

> We were the only two women on the team for two years, and we were each other's support system—and we were friends. I told her I had an idea that I thought would solve a problem our team was dealing with, and I told her I was depending on her to back me up on this. Then, when we went into the meeting, before I could say anything, she pops up and says *she* has a great idea! But it was *my* idea! It floored me! I was devastated. She could at least have said, "Alice and I were talking," and included me, but she didn't. Everyone thought she was great, and she got a promotion out of it. I was so upset. Afterward, I tried to ask her why she did that, but she wouldn't talk to me. I think men do that to each other all the time and they just let it go and move on. We never talked again and she was never my friend again.

Yes, this is a story about a personal betrayal. But it is also a story about women's friendship rules crashing into the norms of a "man's world" where a friendship between two women is destroyed by behavior that is expected between men and rewarded by the organization. A lot has been written about the ways that most workplaces favor and reward masculine workplace values and discourage feminine workplace values, which are described in table 2.

Alice, who worked in an engineering environment, would have found herself right at home in a study conducted by Joyce Fletcher.[7] Fletcher found that the relational practices (which include collaboration, teamwork, coaching, and empathy) preferred by the women engineers in her study were discouraged and undervalued by their organizations, even though the engineers produced good results. She observed that work environments in which engineering is highly valued are often characterized by autonomy, self-promotion, and individual heroics—where self-promotion is essential to being seen as competent.

TABLE 2. Comparison of masculine and feminine workplace values[8]

Masculine workplace values	Feminine workplace values
• Task focus	• Community/team focus
• Isolation/autonomy	• Connection
• Independence	• Interdependence
• Competition—individualistic competitive achievement	• Mutuality—achievement of success through collaboration
• Hierarchical authority	• Collectivity/flat structure
• Rational engagement (focus on task, logic, and the bottom line—leave personal matters at the door)	• Emotional engagement (notice body language and process, encourage relationships, share feelings and personal information, show empathy)
• Directive leadership style	• Supportive leadership style

Alice's story, then, gives us an example of women's friendship rules of unswerving loyalty, trustworthiness, and equality clashing with masculine workplace values of autonomy, self-promotion, and individual heroics. The masculine values get rewarded: Alice's coworker got promoted. And let's notice that Alice says that men compete for promotions through individual heroics all the time. They just go out for a beer and move on, but Alice and her coworker were never friends again.

Engineering environments aren't the only workplaces where masculine values are rewarded as the "right way to be." A strong theme emerged in my research about the clash of feminine values with the masculine values of many workplaces. Let's take a look at some ways that the list of core women's friendship rules represents feminine workplace values that can potentially conflict with the norms of the masculine workplace and create confusion.

Show Unswerving Loyalty and Trustworthiness, and Give Unconditional Acceptance

The research participants described the friendship rules of unswerving loyalty, trustworthiness, and unconditional acceptance as an overlapping range of expectations for a friend at work to always be accepting, to be in agreement, and to be there when needed for validation, affirmation, and understanding. One participant, an African American technology manager in her thirties named Cherry, said, "Whether she's a friend or not, I expect a coworker to relate to what I'm going through if she's a woman." She went on to explain that this also means that she doesn't know what to do if a woman colleague doesn't agree with her: "I know how to disagree with a man but not with a woman." Alice, a study participant we met earlier, explained that not only the expectation of agreement but also the expectation of unconditional acceptance can create disappointment or bad feelings between women coworkers:

> If you criticize women for something or point out a problem, their first reaction is, "I thought she was my friend!" You have to be careful how you deliver the message because women tend to get mad when someone who they thought was their friend criticizes them for anything.

Lisa, a white nurse in her thirties, explained that she expects unconditional acceptance from friends at work. She says, "If they like you as a person, they like you as a coworker. They'll either make you feel better or at least not make you feel worse." These expectations make it difficult for women to disagree with each other at work.

Another research finding was the degree of consistency in the core friendship rules across cultures. The Chinese women who participated in my research had very similar experiences. An HR manager in China said,

> I had a manager in Taiwan. She cried at a meeting because I had a different opinion than her. She expected harmony at all times. I apologized to her and that helped a lot with our relationship. Trust started to build.

While harmony is an important theme in many Asian cultures, this participant ascribed her female manager's behavior to her manager being female—consistent with descriptions by Western participants.

Because of our socialization as women, we often do not learn to manage disagreement or conflict with other girls and women. We are supposed to be nice while boys learn to argue about the rules in their games. We learn to be in conflict with girls indirectly or to fly under the radar with our conflict so that adults cannot see that we do not always feel nice, but that, in fact, girls have a normal range of emotions that they are not allowed to express.[9] This can mean that we become adult women who do not know how to deal directly with conflict with other women, even though we might have learned to be quite comfortable engaging in conflict with men. Most women in my study described themselves as very uncomfortable with conflict and admitted that they avoid it, especially with other women, which can have serious implications for our relationships at work. I observed some cultural differences in this pattern, which will be described in chapter 4.

So what are the implications for our relationships when we carry expectations of loyalty and trustworthiness from other women into the hierarchical workplace? Let's consider the implications of expecting agreement from other women as a test of loyalty or trustworthiness in the context of the workplace.

Most organizations utilize teams as a primary structure for organizing work and, while some people do work alone as individual contributors, most people have to participate in a team at work to some degree. One of the principles underlying the value of teamwork is that a diversity of ideas results in better decisions than individuals can make alone. This means that good teamwork requires team members to express a range of ideas before finding convergence on the one they think is best.

In a masculine workplace culture, ideas are often put forward in team settings in a competitive manner as independent contributions, and in fact, individual contributions are what get rewarded in most organizations. Many organizations talk about valuing teamwork, but very few of them have team-based reward systems. In situations where women are in the minority, women often say that they have trouble getting their ideas heard by their male colleagues in team meetings and that often male colleagues will repeat what a woman has just said and get credit for the idea. In a situation like the one where Alice and her coworker (who stole her idea) were the only two women on the team, it seems likely that the need for loyalty and support from the only other woman colleague increases when it feels difficult to be heard—yet as women, we have to play by the men's rules to be promoted. It is easy to see that if one woman colleague in this type of setting has an idea that is in conflict with the other woman colleague's, or if playing by the men's rules means that the loyalty expectation is betrayed, it can feel like a personal betrayal.

When you add to this a lack of skill in dealing with conflict with another woman, the possibility of damage to the relationship is high. In this way, women's unspoken friendship rules and feminine workplace values—expecting loyalty and valuing collaboration—crash into the workplace context that requires disagreement and individual heroics. The possibility increases that women colleagues will feel disappointed or betrayed by another woman on the team and feel that trust is damaged. The problem is that they probably don't recognize that their friendship rules in the context of the "man's world" of the workplace are setting them up to be disappointed. They probably see their conflict as an interpersonal problem that is only about them as individuals. We will take a look at what to do to prevent this common situation later.

Keep Confidences, Share Gossip, Air Problems, and Be a Good Listener

You may notice right away that there is a contradiction between the friendship rules of keeping confidences and sharing gossip. While we will talk more later about the role of gossip in the workplace, there is a natural land mine in this combination of expectations. How can we keep confidences and share gossip at the same time? Yet both of these expectations were important for the study participants in determining whom they could trust at work. "I build trust with you if you keep my confidences and if you share gossip with me—but that gossip might be someone else's confidential information, which I don't think about in my desire to connect with you." Let's take a look at how these two friendship rules are acted out and their implications in the workplace.

Sharing gossip, airing problems, and being a good listener are ways that women connect in and outside the workplace. Connection is a feminine workplace value (table 2) and can help build trust and motivation to be productive. Lois, a white nurse in her fifties, gave this example of airing problems as a relational expectation in a workplace setting:

> The other night, I worked with someone new who was my charge nurse for that shift. She told me that she's got a set of twins— one's got Down syndrome and is autistic, and the other one has Asperger's—and she has another little girl, too. I thought, "Oh, my God. I just met you and you're telling me all this stuff!" But I kind of felt that I should share something, too, at that point. She told me something. Now I should share something with her. I wanted to share something with her so that she didn't think I was being aloof.

In addition to airing problems, sharing gossip also builds connection and trust—as long as something I have shared in confidence doesn't come back to me as someone else's gossip. Then trust is broken. Masculine workplace values say that having a task focus, demonstrating rational engagement, and working autonomously, without sharing personal information, is the right way to be at work. Women are stereotyped as catty and gossipy, and accused of wasting time when they share personal information and engage in other connecting behaviors, such as listening. I have seen women clients get mediocre performance ratings, even though they reached and exceeded their performance goals, because they "coddled" their direct reports by listening to both their opinions and their personal concerns, as described in the literature.[10] Research on emotional intelligence shows that both women and men respond positively to connection and emotional engagement from their leaders, yet in most organizations, the behaviors of sharing and showing empathy are not rewarded.[11]

The implications for women's relationships in the workplace, when the norms of the workplace reward autonomy and rational engagement rather than women's friendship rules, can be significant. When we expect other women to share gossip and air problems to connect with us and show they are trustworthy yet those behaviors are frowned upon and seen as time wasters by the people who decide on promotions, we learn that we had better not do those things. Then we can be seen as aloof, as Lois described, and other women may not feel they can trust us—and they may not want to support us when we do get rewarded with promotions for playing by the rules of the "man's world." This is one of the many examples of double binds for women in the workplace, which we will spend some time examining in chapter 2. For now, once again, let's notice more ways that we can be set up for disappointment with each other as women working together.

Self-Disclose

The friendship rule of self-disclosure is similar to the rule of airing problems. One additional dimension to this friendship rule is the expectation that emotional expression will be supported by other women. As previously noted, masculine workplace values (table 2) say that we should leave emotions and personal matters at the door when we come to work. It is unlikely that anyone can really do that, woman or man, but you can show emotion at work in limited ways in the masculine workplace. While men can show anger by banging on the table or raising their voices, other emotions are supposed to be suppressed. Tears, in particular, are considered unacceptable at work and are seen as a sign of weakness. One of the study participants explained,

> There's an expectation that you check your feelings at the door.
> "Hey, this is the workplace!" It's not that men don't cry, but
> women are more likely to cry when you hurt their feelings in the
> workplace, and I think it's really hard to cry in the presence of

a man. If you must cry, ask a woman friend to meet you in the restroom and cry with a woman.

Once again, women are set up to be disappointed by each other in the context of the masculine workplace if they expect empathy and emotional engagement from each other, and some women are trying to play by the rules of the masculine workplace to get promoted. Many women in this study, as well as in my consulting and coaching work, have told me how important it is that they not cry at work. Why? Because they will be seen as weak? They will make men uncomfortable? Tears mean you are irrational and out of control? You can't be a leader and cry? These reasons have never made sense to me. Expressing a full range of emotions is part of effective communication and authentic leadership. When women (and men) have to choke off emotion, such as those expressed by tears, they are choking off their ability to fully and authentically express themselves and are suppressing their voice. We will all benefit from working together to change this norm.

Practice Equality

The friendship rule of practicing equality can create confusion for women in the workplace in at least three different situations:

- When we are reluctant to compete with each other for jobs
- When we are reluctant to support each other because a colleague got promoted or has more education
- When we are reluctant to do the self-promotion necessary to get ahead in most organizations

Pat Heim and Susan Murphy call this women's relational expectation the Power Dead-Even Rule.[12] That is, we value (and expect) staying at the same level and not getting ahead of each other. Lois explained why she does not mention that she has a master's degree:

I'm hesitant to say I have a master's degree because it lowers the other person's (woman's) perception of you. She will think, "Who the hell do you think you are?" She will think you're uppity, and she, and others, will be more reticent and not give you information and help. It's important not to appear that you are tooting your own horn.

My clients often talk about their reluctance to apply for a position in their companies when another woman also wants the position because they're concerned about damaging an actual or potential relationship. My study also revealed a strong theme about discomfort with advancing ahead of friends or colleagues and fear or actual experiences of the relationships not surviving such advancements. Of course, part of the problem is that our expectations are unconscious and unspoken, making it impossible to put them on the table and negotiate them. But once again, the feminine workplace values of a flat structure and equality crash into the hierarchical workplace to set us up for disappointment or confusion about what to expect from other women at work. We cannot advance if we don't toot our own horns and compete for promotions, yet this can create problems for our relationships with other women.

Don't Discuss Friendship Rules

The last friendship rule is the "mother of all friendship rules." An unspoken taboo says we cannot name our friendship rules. While it is true that our relationship expectations, or friendship rules, become unconscious by the time we are adults, it is also true that for many of us, when another woman does not behave in the way we expect, our reflex is to stop speaking to her or withdraw from the relationship rather than to talk about what happened. We become distant or cold without explaining why. Or in relationships outside of work, we may stop returning calls and just disappear without an explanation. I have heard every excuse in the book about why women withdraw rather than confront an ex-friend (and yes, I have done this myself). The excuses sound something like this:

- "She should know what she did."
- "I shouldn't have to say anything. She should be able to figure it out."
- "There isn't any point in bringing it up because she would just get defensive."
- "I can't trust her now so what's the point?"

The taboo against discussion means that mismatched assumptions may not be discovered until damage has been done to the relationship. Vana, a Latina manager in the United States in her forties, explained,

> We never really stop and talk about what we expect from each other as friends. I know I would always help you out, but we never stop and say those things. We just, in our minds, expect it—and it's our own fault that we get burned sometimes.

It becomes even more imperative to be able to name and discuss our friendship rules in the workplace, where boundary and role confusion also enter the picture. We must learn to articulate and negotiate our friendship rules and develop relational courage so that we can stay present and in relationships when other women do not meet our expectations.[13]

NEXT STEPS

The exercises below are designed to raise your awareness about your organization, your friendship rules, and your own mind-set about conflict. We suggest some action steps you can take to get others around you to start thinking about these issues and to begin a dialogue that can lead to change.

1. Assess your organization's culture.

   a. Describe your organization's culture using table 2 in this chapter. Which values are rewarded? Which values are discouraged? Which values best fit your own orientation to the world?

   b. Share your perceptions with other colleagues and, possibly, with your boss.

2. Identify your friendship rules. Talk to your friends, coworkers, and family members and bring these rules into your consciousness. Write them down. Continue to notice your unspoken expectations.

3. Identify the friendship rules of other women in your life, both inside and outside of work. Help bring these rules into their consciousness. Begin to notice where yours and theirs are similar and different.

4. Become more comfortable with conflict.

    a. Make a list of the thoughts and feelings that come up for you when you think about conflict. Notice whether you think about conflict as negative or neutral.

    b. The next time a conflict or potential disagreement comes up, take the risk to reframe it as just a difference of opinion and stay engaged. Notice what happens.

    c. Assess how your organization holds or values conflict. Is conflict seen as healthy or as destructive? Is it encouraged or discouraged? Compare your perceptions with your coworkers and, possibly, with your boss.

2

You Can't Get Too Buddy-Buddy with Women:
Double Binds and Limited Support

Are you my friend or my boss?

It hurts my heart when women get a bad rap as bosses. My experiences with female bosses have been good, for the most part, and I have tried to be a good supervisor myself. The relational skills that we learn as girls should serve us well when we become adults and are bosses. But reports of women saying they prefer working for a man are very common not only in the Western media but also among the participants in my research who are located in China, Mexico, and Spain.[1] Could our unconscious women's friendship rules be clashing with masculine work cultures and setting us up for disappointment with women bosses? Let's take a look at a story from Rosa, an HR manager in her forties in Spain, and see what light it sheds:

> I was excited about starting my new job because for the first time, my boss was a woman. I felt sure we would "talk the same language" as women, which was such a relief after my struggles at my previous job. On the first day, my new boss invited me to coffee, which seemed like such a great start! It wasn't long,

though, before she called me into her office and got angry with me about how I handled an assignment. I left the meeting chagrined and confused and ran into my colleague, Anna, who said, "The problem is that she's a woman and we are women. Sometimes she is a friend and sometimes she's the boss."

I said, "I wish she were a man. Then I would know what to expect."

"Me, too," said Anna.

Where do these different expectations for female and male bosses come from? Sheri, a white technology manager in the US in her forties, explained her expectation this way:

I worked for a woman who was more task focused, and it did drive me away. With a guy, I would have expected it, but I expected a little bit more of a relationship from her. It was all she could do to say, "How was your weekend?" It just killed her to say it, and that made it real uncomfortable for me. If a guy did it, I guess it wouldn't bother me as much.

These different expectations for male and female bosses can create double binds for women. Let's take a look now at how double binds are at play for female supervisors.

Double Binds for Female Bosses

Both Rosa and Sheri expected more of a relationship with their female bosses than they expected of male bosses. They expected their male supervisors to be more task focused. Yet consider the double bind that this sets up for female supervisors. As we saw in table 2, the masculine workplace values that are rewarded are task focus and autonomy. On the one hand, female bosses are expected to demonstrate task focus and independent behavior to get good evaluations from their bosses. On the other hand, feminine workplace values (table 2) and women's friendship rules (table 1) set up an expectation for women to build connection through sharing and listening to build trust. Hence, the double bind, also known as the "damned if you do and damned if you don't" situation that female bosses can find themselves in at work.

It might seem that the simplest thing to do if you are a female boss is to adopt a masculine style and stay aloof from your female employees. However, research shows the importance of relational skills for effective leadership, and staying aloof as a female leader can backfire.[2] Not only might it set up the other women at your workplace to feel uncomfortable with you, as Sheri described, but it might also demotivate them and affect their productivity. Shantel, a white American technology supervisor in her forties, explained that she has a natural masculine style that can create problems for her with female employees. "If you come in and seem too cool and not interested, that can be a disadvantage," she explained. She has been told by her manager that she has to do more to increase morale among her female team members because they complain about her style and don't like working for her. Shantel feels that she will have to chat more with the women to raise morale because they "value chatting," which she isn't thrilled about but she will have to take the time to do—something not expected from her male peers.

Like Shantel, many women come into the workplace with a masculine style that fits nicely with masculine workplace values but can run afoul of women's friendship rules. Women with a masculine style may not feel comfortable chatting, or self-disclosing and asking about someone else's family or outside life. Many of these women, especially if they are not parents, find it as difficult to engage in conversations with women about their children as they do to talk about football with the men in the office. In addition, cultural differences might mean that sharing or asking someone else to share personal information in the workplace is not comfortable. For example, Sonja, a technology manager from the Middle East who is in her forties, explained that asking personal questions is not acceptable for anyone in her culture. She might tell a coworker something personal if she or he *doesn't* ask, "but if you ask me, I'm not going to tell you," she said. This is another way in which—when we leave our friendship rules unspoken—we could be wrong about how we interpret another woman's behavior and thereby limit our working relationship.

This same topic raised a lot of hackles among a group of women participating in this study in Spain. When one of the participants, Graciella, a financial services manager in her forties, described her approach to being a boss, an uproar erupted from the group. Graciella explained, "If I'm the manager, I don't care about your personal problems—whether you are a woman or a man. I don't want to be involved in your life. It's not part of my job." The objections were loud from the women in the group, and a lively discussion ensued about how being friendly makes it easier to get things done at work and having good relationships creates a better work environment. When Graciella was asked to say more about her professional experience, she acknowledged that female staff don't stay long on her teams and that she had been told she was hard to work for—although she had never thought about the possibility that female staff had different expectations of her than of her male colleagues.

Many female clients have complained that it's more difficult for them to get things done when working with female staff than is true for their male colleagues. As Rosa and Sheri described in the first part of this chapter, women expect more investment in relationships from female bosses and superiors. If those expectations are not met, they could feel less motivated to cooperate. Complicating matters for female bosses is the friendship rule about practicing equality, or the Power Dead-Even Rule described by Pat Heim and Susan Murphy.[3] The Power Dead-Even Rule is the invisible "natural law" (or friendship rule) that says, "For a positive relationship to be possible between two women, the self-esteem and power of one must be, in the perception of each woman, similar in weight to the self-esteem and power of the other."[4] This friendship rule sets us up to feel uncomfortable with women who have more status and power or who toot their own horn and get promoted. The combination of the Power Dead-Even Rule and the expectation of women bosses to be more relational, which is not rewarded in the masculine workplace, sets us up for confusion and frustration about what to expect from female bosses, as well as confusion about how to be a female boss in the hierarchical workplace.

Because of women's relational and equality expectations, female supervisors need to engage in "leveling" by being relational (chatting) with their female staff to counteract the reflex reaction that can occur when a woman has more status. In this case, we are talking about leveling as intentionally practicing self-disclosure, empathy, and listening in the workplace, but most women know well how to level with women in another way. For example, when was the last time a woman paid you a compliment, such as "I love your outfit," and you responded by saying something like "Oh, this old thing? I've had it for years," or "I bought it on sale and it cost practically nothing"? This is leveling, too. I catch myself making leveling responses, or otherwise making it clear that I do not see myself as being better or having more than another woman, on a regular basis, and I notice this as my deeply embedded reflex for how to stay on positive terms with other women.

While we need to be concerned about the percentage of women reporting that they prefer working for a man, not all women dislike having female bosses. Many women in my study, as well as many female clients, report feeling supported by female bosses in a way they do not experience with men. These women said that female bosses were more likely to understand their struggles about deciding when to start a family and were often more understanding about their needing time off for children's events or for caring for aging parents. Laurie, a white manager in her forties in the travel industry, described her positive experience:

> When I worked for a woman, she was more willing to listen. We were able to disclose and discover that we had similar challenges in the male-dominated business world, which made our relationship special. We were able to shore each other up, I guess.

Where is the line for female bosses about how friendly to be with their female staff? We will explore some of the dilemmas and pitfalls for female bosses in chapter 3. Because women's expectations of relationship and equality conflict with the hierarchical norms of the masculine workplace, it is easy to see the double bind for female bosses and why many women say they prefer working for men. Our expectations of men are so much simpler—all task, no relationship.

Other Double Binds

Another double bind that many women face in organizations is that they are in a lose-lose situation when they are the only woman on a team, as described by Alice:

> It's (the organization) just so political and still male dominated. But you know, I tended to be able to keep up with them, and give them one for one back, but it wasn't comfortable for me. There were eight men on the team and I was the only woman. It was a constant battle, and I almost had to be perceived as a bitch to get my point across—and then I was perceived as a bitch.

Alice gives us an example of the double bind for women who adopt masculine behaviors to try to fit in and be successful in the masculine workplace. She could "give them one for one back," which she had to do to get her ideas heard, but then she was "perceived as a bitch."

Research has shown that women are really never allowed to adopt a masculine style in the same way that men are allowed to adopt a feminine style without being seen as dominating or aggressive.[5] Kathy, a white technology manager in her thirties, provides another example of women not being allowed to adopt a masculine style:

> They say that men interrupt each other all the time and women don't. If I'm in a meeting and I interrupt, I get in trouble, but I don't see men get in trouble for that. I'll be in a meeting and if I interrupt, my manager will tell me, "You were interrupting." But if other men were in there interrupting each other, not a word from him. They say that women don't do it, but when you do, it's seen as very aggressive and inappropriate behavior.

Think about how harshly Hillary Clinton was judged for being too ambitious and aggressive when she ran for president of the United States in 2008. I sometimes thought that women judged her more harshly than men did for behaving like a man and tooting her own horn in her attempts to win the election. She had to shed tears in a public forum—in other words, behave like a woman by showing emotion—for many people to soften toward her enough to consider voting for her.

Sheryl Sandberg, in her book *Lean In*, makes the point that women cannot ignore the many double binds they face in the workplace if they want to be successful, however they may define success.[6] She makes a strong case and cites solid research about the importance for women of being likeable if they wish to succeed and the double bind this creates for women.[7] One of the studies described by Sandberg was conducted by two professors who used a Harvard Business School case study that described a real-life entrepreneur. They gave the case to business-school students to rate on several factors. Half the students got the case with the name Heidi, and the other half got the same case with the name Howard. While the students rated both Heidi and Howard as competent, they rated Howard as a more appealing colleague, while Heidi was seen as "not the type of person you would want to hire or work for."[8]

Sandberg notes that this study shows what many other studies have also shown: "When a man is successful, he is liked by both men and women. When a woman is successful, people of both genders like her less." In other words, "success and likeability are positively correlated for men and negatively correlated for women."[9]

The career implications are obvious. If we cannot get hired or promoted because our competence makes both women and men uncomfortable, we are in big trouble. If we play down our accomplishments and do not toot our own horn about our capabilities to level and be likeable, we cannot get access to opportunities. An additional research finding shows that one reason women are paid less than men for the same work is that women do not try to negotiate for compensation, benefits, titles, and other perks as often as men do. But as Sandberg points out, women have a good reason for not negotiating.[10] We have learned that if we advocate for ourselves, we are often seen as too demanding or aggressive and not someone people want to hire or promote.

The literature contains many suggestions about what women can do to be both likeable and successful during negotiations, which include smiling a lot and, in the case of Hillary Clinton, crying in public to make people more comfortable with her as a woman competing for a "man's role"— president.[11] I hope to see the day when women do not have to worry about being liked any more than men have to think about that to be successful—or when both women and men care a lot about being liked—but for now, we do have to play by a different and more complicated set of rules.

The easiest way to start reducing the confusion and double binds for women is for women to become aware of our unconscious gender-based expectations of each other and to start challenging ourselves and each other to be more supportive of women at all levels in the workplace. By supporting each other, we will be able to accelerate the rate of advancement of women into the upper levels of organizations, where we can gain critical mass to expand the range of behaviors that are valued and rewarded and eliminate the double binds. Which brings us to the question, why aren't women more supportive of each other in the workplace?

Limited Support from Women—Why Does It Happen?

Of course, many women do support each other. However, too often women do not feel supported by other women at work. Our focus here is on why support doesn't happen so that we can find pathways to changing this dynamic.

Women Are Discouraged from Supporting Other Women

One of my first jobs after college was as a researcher in a small mental health research institute where about half the staff was female and the senior leaders were both men. At that point, I had been active in various social movements, including the women's liberation movement, for several years and had learned about the importance, for me, of women supporting each other. As I was newly hired and in need of support, I did what I knew how to do and organized the other female staff to go out for a "women's lunch" so that we could get to know each other better. When word got back to the men in senior management that the women were going out to lunch together for the first time, all hell broke loose! I was surprised at their reaction—we were just going out to lunch—but we were ordered to cancel our plans. Not only did we not go out to lunch, but the other women barely spoke to me for the rest of my tenure at the institute. They appeared to have gotten the message from the male leaders that being too friendly with the other women was not good for their careers, and I was a person who had dangerous ideas that were, somehow, threatening to the established order.

What happened to me is part of the story about why women don't support each other more at work. Women are discouraged from supporting each other in the masculine hierarchical workplace for a variety of reasons. The first reason is an obvious one when you consider that there are very few women at the top. Only 3 percent of Fortune 500 CEOs are women, a percentage that also holds true for CEOs in nonprofit and government organizations.[12] In addition, only 14 percent of executives at Fortune 500 companies and 18 percent of elected officials in the United States are women.[13] The gap is much worse for women of color.[14] When very few women are at the top, predominantly men control the rewards. Grace, a white technology manager in her fifties, one of my research participants, explained that it is easier for women "at the bottom of the pyramid" to support each other. She said that when women move into more senior positions,

> You're playing a game with men because there are no women at the top—so you can't get too buddy-buddy with women because that takes away from your ability to climb the corporate ladder.

She went on to explain that because there are few women at the top, men need to see you as a team player. In other words, they need to feel comfortable that you are going to be able to fit in as "one of the boys" and will not threaten the established order. Shantel, another research participant, explained why she does not participate in women's support activities at her company:

I work in a very male-dominated profession, and my goal is to learn to operate within that environment. I have trouble being interested in "the women's this" and "the women's that" because my life is focused on how can I get recognized and rewarded by the guys.[15]

One problem with having to focus on being rewarded by men is that not only do women not see value in supporting other women, but we twist ourselves to fit into a masculine culture to the point that we lose touch with our own voice and our own feelings.[16] We suppress our own experience to be acceptable to those with power, and we can lose touch with aspects of our authentic experience. When facilitating gender-awareness workshops, I often find that the women actually argue louder than the men about the absence of differences in their organizational experiences and opportunities for women and men. This resistance usually melts away after the women talk with each other for a while in a same-gender group and share stories during the workshop. Maureen Walker talks about the pattern of women distancing themselves from other women as a strategy of disconnection that women (and other devalued groups) use for survival.[17] Adult women disconnect from each other in organizations to make men comfortable. If the men feel uncomfortable, the backlash can mean that promotions and other rewards are withheld from the women.[18] Metaphorically, lunch can get cancelled.

Another possible reason why women do not support each other more is that when women support other women, the male leadership may see this as being weak. Study participants like Susan, a white COO in her thirties in a consulting firm, explained that in her organization, she and some other women want to "support other women and bring them up," but they recognize that it's a risk to do that. She says, "If you go over to the women's group, the men will see you as weak and won't think you can 'play the male role.'" This type of perceived weakness could damage your career if you are seen as not being able to make tough decisions. This is probably a reflection of the stereotype of women as weak and men as strong, which requires women to prove they can be one of the boys by maintaining their distance from other women so that their ability to make tough decisions isn't weakened by having good relationships.

There Are Limited Spaces at the Top

The fact that so few women are in senior leadership roles creates another dynamic for women that inhibits support: the perception that women must compete against each other for the limited slots available for women. One of the research participants, Cherry, a technology manager, explained why she does not think that men need support to advance in the same way that women need support: "There are a lot more spaces for men than there are for women." In other words, men just have more opportunity to advance. Because the number of jobs for women at the top is so low and the percentage of women in senior management has been stagnant for so long—at least the last ten years—it is easy to understand how women may see each other as competitors for the limited number of positions available. Laurie, a white manager in her forties in the travel industry, explained her viewpoint in this way:

> You see the successful women as your competition. You don't really see the whole pie or all the people out there as your competition. I think it's easier to compete one on one with a woman than with a man.

Scholars have described the mind-set reflected by Cherry and Laurie as "a dearth mentality," or the feeling that there is not enough to go around.[19] This mind-set could explain why we can sometimes feel that other women are our competition. Marissa, a white government supervisor in her fifties, explained:

> Very sadly, I see it a lot in the upper levels of government that women try to do each other in. Women, when they are promoted, will tend to be appointed at the lower end of the salary scale for their position, while the men almost always come in at the top of the scale. Women will try to do each other in at that upper level if another woman starts at a higher salary than they did. You certainly don't want some other woman doing better than you.

So if a woman comes in at a higher salary, the other women try to undermine her. These women don't try to undermine the men for routinely getting hired at the top of the salary scale. Could it be that women go after each other because the dearth mentality says there isn't enough to go around for women? If we combine the friendship rule of equality, which says we all have to be the same, with the dearth mentality, then a desire to be supportive is probably not the emotion that gets triggered if another woman seems to be doing better than we are. The women in China who participated in this research confirmed that the same dynamic exists in both Western and Chinese companies. Zung, a manager in her thirties, explained, "Women give you a lot of attention when you are young, but as soon as you become more senior and a possible competitor, they stop supporting you."

We will consider other implications for women of limited spaces at the top, such as career sabotage, in a later chapter. For now, let's keep the focus on why support doesn't happen.

The dearth mentality can also result in women, and members of other socially devalued groups, going out of their way not to give special treatment to those like them—and often even treat them more harshly.[20] Sometimes this decision is conscious, but it is probably more often unconscious. In an article in a special section of the *New York Times* in April 2013, entitled "Women in a Man's World," female executives on Wall Street were interviewed and asked why so few women had made it to the senior ranks. In interview after interview, the female executives blamed themselves for not trying to change the status quo. One of the executives, Irene Dorner, the chief executive of HSBC USA, explained that throughout her career she had "kept her head down, focusing on her own career."[21] She acknowledged that she and the other female executives in the financial industry had not been very good role models and had not spoken out or complained about misogynistic comments and discriminatory practices.

The executive women interviewed for the *New York Times* article were usually the only women at their levels in their companies.[22] Having limited spaces at the top means that the few women who are there can't change things alone, so the status quo can continue undisturbed. The junior women in a company may believe a senior woman is choosing not to do anything to help other women when the truth is that the senior woman may feel that her hands are tied. The pressure for lone women who make it to the top to keep their focus on proving themselves to the men, while not being perceived as threatening, is intense.

Fortunately, more and more organizations are developing support structures, such as mentoring and sponsorship programs, women's leadership training and networking events, and other forums to create spaces for women to build connections and gain access to opportunities. Sponsorship programs, in particular, are now focusing at cracking the glass ceiling at the executive level for women. Research shows that women with the same education as their male counterparts, hired at the same time in the same roles, reported significantly less income, job satisfaction, and advancement within a few years of beginning their careers.[23] The research reveals that the men often receive sponsorship or advocacy, while the women receive mentoring. A mentor is someone who gives you advice. A sponsor is someone who pulls you along and gets you access to opportunities. Because there are more men at the top and we all naturally sponsor those with whom we feel most comfortable, men tend to sponsor younger men. Women do not have the same access to sponsorship without a formal program that structures sponsorship into an organization's practices. Many senior women, along with senior men, are supporting the creation of these new programs and structures, which means that executive women will no longer have the pressure to change things alone.

We have considered several reasons why women don't support each other more in the workplace. Different expectations of female bosses that conflict with the hierarchical norms of the masculine workplace, double binds for women managers with masculine styles, organizational practices and reward systems that discourage women from supporting each other, and the impact on women's relationships of limited spaces for women at the top are some of the issues involved. All of these issues can be addressed and changed—if we support each other more and join together to make changes. We can do this, but we must begin by being honest with ourselves about our own expectations of women and challenge ourselves to acknowledge and break unconscious patterns.

NEXT STEPS

Reflect on your expectations of your bosses in the activities below and rate yourself on some basic dimensions of support for women and women leaders. These exercises can start you on a path to being more supportive of other women in ways you may not be aware of now.

1. Make a list that describes the characteristics of your ideal boss, in general. Then make a list that describes your ideal woman boss. Once you have your lists, compare them. What do you notice? What friendship rules might be operating for you with your ideal woman boss?

2. Be honest with yourself, and put a check mark by the statements below that apply to you. We have all participated in many of these behaviors at some point. Notice them as you go forward and challenge yourself to stop doing them.

   Have you ever

   ☐ Laughed at a joke told by a man at the expense of a woman?

   ☐ Assumed a woman got promoted because of whom she slept with?

   ☐ Assumed a woman got a job because of a quota?

   ☐ Talked about other women with men to be accepted as "one of the boys"?

   ☐ Said another woman was too sensitive about gender issues?

   ☐ Been more critical of women leaders than of men?

   ☐ Said, "I hate working for women"?

   ☐ Consciously undermined a woman leader?

Use the following scoring guide to reflect upon your answers:

1–2 checks = You are relatively supportive of other women.

3–4 checks = You are somewhat less supportive of other women.

5+ checks = You have a strong tendency to not be supportive of other women.

3. Notice your reflex to be critical or dismissive of other women, especially if they are successful. Ask a buddy to do this exercise with you. When you each notice the reflex to be critical or dismissive of other women, mark it down in a notebook or electronic notepad. Share your marks with each other weekly to help each other see patterns and raise your awareness.

3

One Ball of Wax:
Avoiding Boundary Confusion

Am I your boss or your friend?

Where is the line for female bosses about how friendly to be with their female staff? Personally, I have friendships that have lasted for decades with people who were my senior leaders or my direct reports. But many of the women in my research and in my audiences express genuine confusion about how to handle this boundary. They are unsure about where to draw the line or how to manage the relational expectations of their female staff. One of the research participants, Penny, who is a white administrator in her fifties in higher education, shared this example of one impact of boundary confusion from the point of view of female staff:

> Women superiors invite us all to share our feelings about things
> without any recognition that there's a hierarchy present in the
> room. And you leave the room and then all you've said is held
> against you. So it's almost like, "All right, let's be women. All
> right, now we're in business, keeping score." Let's be women.
> Let's all share our feelings, and let's be equal, and we don't like
> hierarchy, and we think we should all be on the same level. We're

not comfortable with hierarchy, but it still is a factor that's not recognized in the room. It's like a trick. It's like luring you in under the guise of being all women together, and then what you share is held against you going forward in the company.

Penny's example shows the clashing of women's friendship rules, such as self-disclosure and practicing equality, with the hierarchical workplace and the confusion that can occur for both female bosses and female staff about what to expect from each other, compounded by the taboo against discussing friendship rules. Now let's consider what's positive about boundary confusion between women at work. We will return to the problematic side later.

Women Have Fluid Boundaries

One cause of boundary confusion is having fluid boundaries, which is also one of our strengths as women. Fluid boundaries allow for relationships to be central in our lives, both at work and outside work. Linda, a white technology manager in her forties who took part in the research, explained it this way: "I think it's just female nature that you don't have all these separations. Your professional relationships and your personal relationships are all in one ball of wax."

The Positive Side of Fluid Boundaries

Scholars agree with Linda that women tend to emphasize the fluid nature of the boundaries between personal life and work life.[1] Fluid boundaries make sense if you consider the feminine workplace values of community, mutuality, connection, and emotional engagement—not to mention the friendship rules of self-disclosure and equality. Relationships between women at work provide support, validation, mentoring, and empowerment—all of which have been shown to be essential to women's mental and emotional health in male-dominated work environments.[2] Remember the example in chapter 2 about the female employee and her female boss who discovered, through disclosure to each other, that "we had similar challenges in the male-dominated business world… We were able to shore each other up."

For female bosses, some fluidity in boundaries is necessary to meet the relational expectations of female staff, as described in the double bind discussion in chapter 2. Fluid boundaries make sense for other reasons as well. For example, as human beings we grow and develop throughout our lives, both inside and outside the workplace. Judith Jordan, a feminist scholar who studies the centrality of relationships in our lives, writes that "we need connections to flourish."[3] She explains that human connection and relationship are central to our growth and development. Something both she and other scholars call "growth-fostering relationships" are the key.[4]

In the context of the workplace, a boss needs to support the growth and development of her employees not only to foster productivity but also to continue to grow and learn herself through her interactions with her staff. Growth-fostering relationships, then, require mutual empathy and mutual empowerment between boss and subordinates, as well as among peers, which cannot happen without some fluidity in role boundaries. The payoff for everyone is increased energy, creativity, and productivity—and better teamwork.[5] The trick is to leverage the best of what fluid boundaries have to offer—growth-fostering relationships— while learning to prevent the negative impacts of fluid boundaries that can also occur.

The Negative Side of Fluid Boundaries

Let's take a closer look now at the negative impacts of fluid boundaries and some strategies for preventing them.

Confusion for Staff

In the opening story of this chapter, Penny described one type of boundary confusion from a staff perspective when she told of women bosses who seem to expect personal disclosure that was then used against the disclosers. Her description included sharing of feelings in an all-woman space, where relationship matters, that was then used in a business or hierarchical space where "keeping score" is what matters. This felt to Penny like being tricked by her women bosses and left her wondering whom she could trust.

Another example of boundary confusion from a staff perspective comes from a research participant in China. Jang, a human resources manager in her forties, explained that women bosses seem to use relationship as a standard for evaluating the performance of women employees:

> With women bosses, we talk about kids, husbands, vacations, fashion, and more emotional things. With men, we only talk about work. With a female leader, things don't depend on your performance; they depend on your relationship with her and her feelings toward you. I've heard other women say they prefer working for a male boss because men are more fair and objective.

It is worth noting that while Asian cultures are known to be more relationship based than is generally true in US culture, the Chinese participants in this study still ascribed key differences in boundary confusion to gender differences.[6] It seems possible that both women's friendship rules and feminine workplace values are being reflected in Jang's statement.

Both Ilena, in her twenties, and Angella, in her thirties, managers in Mexico, expressed similar sentiments about female bosses. They said that women are more difficult to work with than men because men are more task focused. Ilena also described another situation, from a staff perspective, where relationship expectations across role boundaries were confused because the boss didn't manage them well. Ilena felt she had to pretend to be friends with a female boss because that is what the boss expected and the boss had more power. Ilena's boss expected her to act like a friend, which included lots of self-disclosure and socializing outside of work. Once the woman moved to a different department, Ilena explained "I don't have to be her friend anymore because she's no longer my boss." We can see in this case how the mixing of fluid boundaries and hierarchical status differences can create pressure for staff to fake a relationship when the awareness and skills for managing the boss-employee role boundary are absent.

From a staff perspective, a lack of clarity about role boundaries, or the inability to name and negotiate them while staying in the relationship, means that women can experience disappointment or confusion about the behavior of women bosses. Female staff can feel tricked or pressured by women bosses or feel that their performance is being evaluated unfairly. None of these outcomes needs to happen.

Confusion for Bosses

Let's return to Penny, the administrator in higher education who felt tricked by her female bosses. Penny explained that now that she is the boss, she feels the double bind caused by the clash of women's friendship rules and the hierarchical workplace culture:

> My women staff will come to me and say, "How's your boyfriend?" They feel like a relationship with me should be all access, and I don't want to set up a situation where I'm becoming this kind of friend with them—not just a friend but an intimate friend. We tell all. Then all of a sudden I've got to be the person who says, "Get that done. Get it done tonight." Then that's a betrayal of womanhood to assert my authority when it's going to cost them something.

In chapter 2, we considered the negative consequences for female bosses when they are too distant or aloof and do not meet the relational expectations of their female staff. Letitia, a white technology manager in her forties, explained the dilemma that Penny faces as the boss: "It's as though they expect you to subordinate the boss-subordinate relationship to the woman-friend relationship. They would not ask that of a man."

What is the answer? Both scholars and about 25 percent of the women in this study propose that women learn to make a distinction between being friends and being friendly with women at work, especially when they are the boss.[7] I would go a step further and say that it does not need to be an either/or option—that we can be both friends and friendly as the boss, but we need to be able to name whether we are the boss or a friend in any given interaction, with a clear understanding of how the relational rules or expectations are different in each situation. Kathy, a technology manager, explained how this approach works for her:

> I do have two women I was friends with before I was promoted to management. I think we do a wonderful job of saying, "All right, this is a professional conversation." If it's a professional conversation, they know there are some things I cannot talk about. And if it's not a professional conversation anymore, we are also clear with each other about that.

When Kathy says the women are clear about when they are having a professional conversation and when they are not, this means that she and her friends have specified where the boundaries are for each of them in a professional conversation. In other words, they have specified what they can and cannot talk about in their professional roles so that the expectations are clear. More details about a tool to accomplish this type of successful boundary management will be described later in this chapter. But before we go there, let's take a look at a type of boundary confusion that can be particularly destructive if not handled well: when a friend becomes your boss.

When a Friend Becomes the Boss

Another type of boundary confusion that is fairly common happens between two friends who were either coworkers at the same level or were friends outside the workplace context and one friend becomes the boss of the other. Kate, a white manager in her twenties in a financial services organization, describes this experience for her:

> I have two close women friends at work, and one of them—it was announced last week—now reports to me. I feel somewhat upset because I think she's upset. I feel she used to look to me as a friend, and now it's like, "Oh, gosh. You're my boss!" She was instant-messaging me the day we found out. She was asking, "Did you know about this?" She came to my house Saturday. I mean, we're friends! I would never, ever want to upset her by any means. And I was a little bit upset that she thought I would know about something like that and not tell her.

There is trouble ahead for these two friends if they do not talk about how this change in their roles at work means their friendship expectations need to change. Kate will not be able to tell her friend everything about confidential information she will have as the boss. If the two women can name and negotiate their expectations for how they will deal with professional topics that come up versus when they are just being friends, they will be able to continue being close friends. If not, the consequences could be disastrous for them professionally or personally or both.

A recent example of the kind of trouble Kate may be facing with her friend if they don't learn to manage the changes in their roles comes from a new coaching client in my practice. This client, Stephanie, a white woman in her twenties who is a union executive, hired me as her coach because she was recently promoted and her good friend, a man, now reports to her. He is upset because he was not promoted, and she feels guilty and thinks she must prove her loyalty to him and their friendship. She has shown her loyalty by telling him information she now hears in her new position, and she has also pushed him into the limelight in some situations where she was supposed to be the one there. Her boss is disappointed in her and is now questioning whether she is willing, or able, to step into her new leadership role. He wants her to cut off the friendship with her colleague and distance herself from him. Stephanie feels stuck. Without the intervention of her coach, she might lose her promotion or damage the friendship or both—but neither needs to happen. Later in this chapter, we will take a look at the tool, role hats, that Stephanie is learning to use. But first, let's consider some other ways that problems can develop when a friend becomes the boss.

The following is the story of two good friends who did not handle the changes in their roles well, so their friendship was destroyed, as related by Jane, a white technology manager in her thirties:

> I went to work for a friend and she would actually overstep her professional boundaries. She wouldn't think anything of calling me late at night on my time. Normally, before she was my boss, we would just have friendly chats at night, but now she would give me tasks to do late at night. She also wouldn't think anything

of saying to me during the workday, "Hey, do you mind going and picking up my son and bringing him back to me?" It's funny, we had an administrative person, but she would never think to ask her to do that stuff for her.

Then I got an offer outside the company and I told her. She really took it personally. She acted like I was betraying her instead of being happy that I had such a great new opportunity. I was so hurt and disappointed.

When Jane went to work for her friend, do you think they talked about their friendship rules and how they would need to change as they moved into new boss and employee roles with each other? Or how they were going to manage the boss-subordinate friendship boundaries? Not unusually, they did not. Jane's boss continued to behave as though she and Jane were still equals, which they were not. Her power over Jane meant that Jane did not feel she could say no to her boss's workday requests or late-night calls. Behaviors that are appropriate between friends, such as chatting on the phone at night, crossed the line for Jane when the calls became about work. With no recognition of the change in their roles and no way to name and negotiate the friend-boss boundaries, Jane felt taken advantage of. Her boss, then, felt betrayed by Jane when her expectation of loyalty from Jane as a friend ran afoul of Jane's opportunity for professional advancement—a situation where a boss should have been supportive. Not surprisingly, the friendship did not survive.

In another example of the confusion that can occur when a friend becomes the boss and the two friends don't know how to talk about their new roles, Justine, a white technology manager in her forties, describes her challenge as the employee:

I went to work for someone who was my friend, and it was hard to bridge those two worlds of working for your friend who is also your leader. I had a lot of fun working with her because we already had a good rapport, but it was hard when she had to discipline, coach, or counsel me. It was hard because she would say, "Come on now." I would say things like, "Are you serious? Are you reprimanding me?" I would never do that in any other professional relationship. I would take in the comments as feedback, I'd probe, and I would question for understanding. In that relationship, it's almost like I questioned my friend's authority. It's hard to switch the light on and off.

Friendships are too important to women's health and survival in organizations to be either minimized, eliminated, or destroyed, yet boundary confusion can be detrimental to our relationships. Table 3 summarizes some consequences of boundary confusion for women colleagues.

TABLE 3. Common consequences of boundary confusion

For staff

- Boundary confusion can damage trust with a boss: "Will she use personal information against me?"
- Staff can feel pressured by a boss to be friends.
- Staff can feel pressured by a boss to accept violations of private off-duty time.
- Staff can perceive that the boss will base performance evaluations on how she feels about the relationship.

For bosses

- Female bosses are in a double bind—they must meet the relational expectations of female staff to be trusted and to motivate staff and they must exercise hierarchical authority.
  - Staff may be demotivated if the boss is not relational enough.
  - If too relational, the boss may have difficulty getting the respect she needs to exercise her authority as the boss.

For friendships—when a friend becomes the boss

- The relational expectations need to change and be clear when roles change. If not, relationships and careers can be damaged.
  - Guilt can get in the way of working together well.
  - Misunderstandings can ruin relationships.
  - Inappropriate information could be shared.

Women coworkers, whether boss and subordinate or peers, need a conscious system of switching between "friend" and "coworker or boss" to enable them to manage the boundary, or know when and how to "switch the light on and off." In the following section, we will consider a tool for managing this switch called "role hats."

Role Hats: A Boundary Negotiation Tool

Women can learn to consciously use a tool adapted from an African American speech practice called "code switching" or "style switching." For our purposes here, we will call this tool "role hats." Scholars describe the practice of code switching used by African Americans as intentionally changing styles of speaking in different environments.[8] For example, consciously switching between Black English and US Standard English was sometimes necessary for survival and for access to jobs and education.

Like code switching, the tool of role hats must be consciously and intentionally used. Unlike code switching, however, the tool of role hats must be intentionally understood and agreed to by all parties. The challenge is that women's friendship rules say it is taboo for women to discuss their relational expectations. Consequently, many women have not developed the skill of naming their relationship expectations to manage their work boundaries. But some women, such as Kathy, have worked out a system similar to naming role hats. Kathy and her friends were able to state when they were in a professional conversation versus a friendship conversation.

More examples of successful boundary management were described by some of the lesbian women in this study. These women described a need to be vigilant about personal and relational boundary management in the workplace. They cannot afford to have their behaviors misinterpreted by heterosexual women colleagues or homophobic bosses and coworkers if they are out as lesbians and they are perceived as being too friendly. It may not be surprising, then, that one of the clearest examples of good boundary management using the role hats tool came from an African American lesbian, Sharon, who was a participant in this study.

Sharon, a senior manager in the healthcare sector in her sixties, described how her early bosses taught her to manage the boss-employee boundary:

> To be friends at work requires total transparency—you must be totally honest on both sides of the boundary. It cannot work to be the senior or the junior person if you cannot trust that what you are seeing is what you are getting.
>
> I explicitly name the role that I'm coming from—which hat I'm wearing—boss or friend. My friend can ask me which hat I'm wearing in any interaction. She can ask me to change hats.
>
> We are always clear about how the role hats are going to work. I am clear with her that when I have my boss hat on, I am speaking from my supervisor role, where I am responsible for the quality of her work—and I may not be happy with it. There may also be things going on in the company that I cannot discuss because of my role, and I will tell her that.
>
> We can also be good friends outside of work, as long as we stay clear about our hats. I have joked that I am friends with bosses and bosses of friends. A friendship may not survive if I have to discipline or fire her—but I've had good luck with that, so it's not always a problem.

"Total transparency"—this, along with the role hats tool, is the key to enable you to "switch the light on and off" to manage role boundaries and relationships at work. Table 4 summarizes the guidelines for using the role hats tool effectively:

Most of us have some experience with naming and negotiating role hats, though we might not have used this term, and we might also be able to enhance our skills. For example, how often have we, as parents, answered a child's question about why she or he has to do something by saying, "Because you're a child, and I'm the adult, and I said so"? This is an example of naming roles, but the relational negotiation is missing. Even with a child, it might be possible to say, "As a grownup, I think you should do this because [give a reason].What do you think you should do?" Feeling that you are interested in her or his opinions and might

TABLE 4. Guidelines for using the role hats tool for boundary negotiation

- Name the roles each person is in, such as boss, friend, colleague or functional role.
- Discuss the needs of each person in each role and really listen to each other (skills: disclosure and empathic listening).
- Offer suggestions to each other for behaviors that could meet each person's needs in each role (skill: mutual coaching).
- Decide on ground rules, or agreements, for how you will both use the role hats, such as:
  - "Ask me which hat I'm wearing."
  - "Ask me to change hats anytime."
- Be honest with each other about whether you can comply with requests and explain why (skills: transparency and mutual empowerment).

be influenced builds confidence and empowerment in a child (or any lower-status person).

A good friend of mine recently asked if I was mad at her because when she called one day I was very curt and crabby, which was uncharacteristic. I realized that our roles had changed in a way that she was unaware of and I had not discussed with her. I had started to write this book and was less available for spontaneous conversations. I thought of my new role as "writer," which now needed to coexist with "friend" because she mattered to me, but we had not talked about how to handle this change. I had answered the phone when I saw her number on the caller ID, but I was in the process of writing and felt interrupted by the call. We needed to discuss how we were going to manage the writer-friend boundary so that we could each get our needs met—and not damage our important relationship. We agreed that either I would tell her when I was having a writing day or I would not answer the phone. I also agreed to call her more often when I was not writing so that she knew when I could talk and knew that I want to stay connected. Not discussing this change could have created a very damaging misunderstanding.

Fluid boundaries can be a strength for women in the workplace. If we can learn to manage our boundaries effectively, we can develop growth-fostering relationships that cross boundaries and result in more energy, more creativity, greater productivity, and better teamwork for all of us. We can be writer and friend, boss and friend, or just friendly colleagues who work well together because we have named and negotiated our relational expectations of each other. But once again, we have to overcome the unconscious taboo/reflex to not talk about our expectations of each other—and we have to name and negotiate our role boundaries where they exist. Imagine how differently things might have gone for Jane and her boss if they had known to use these tools when Jane went to work for her friend. They might still be friends today.

NEXT STEPS

The following exercises will help you develop skills for keeping a relationship healthy when misunderstandings happen or to prevent misunderstandings by keeping role differences clear.

1. Practice the skill of mutual empathy. Identify a relationship, either inside or outside of work, where you have recently experienced some tension that was not discussed.

   a. Write down what you experienced (describe the behaviors you noticed) and what you felt (for example, surprise or discomfort).

   b. Ask the other person for a time to get together to talk something over. Tell her you are concerned that a misunderstanding might have happened. Tell her what you experienced and felt, and ask her what she experienced and felt.

   c. Listen deeply to each other and ask questions for understanding. Do not interrupt each other. Really listen.

2. Practice naming and negotiating. If a misunderstanding was developing in step 1 above, then name the friendship rules that may have been operating for you, and ask the other person how they

compare to hers. Try to agree on new ones that will work better to meet the needs you both have.

3. Practice role hats. The next time you are going to a meeting with a woman who has a role different from yours (with either a level or a functional difference), ask a colleague to help you clarify the roles before the meeting. Write down the role hat you think you will wear and the one the other woman will wear in the upcoming meeting. Debrief with your colleague after the meeting. What did you notice about your expectations for the interaction? Continue this practice before the next few meetings to sharpen your skills.

4

Under Our Breath:
Gossip and Indirect Communication

What's good about gossip?

Sharing gossip is one of our friendship rules (see table 1), and we often expect to talk about other people with each other in friendship interactions. One of the biggest surprises from this study came from a role-play developed and performed by one of the last research groups—a group of managers in state-level government. While gossip was a frequently mentioned topic in many of the group discussions and interviews during this research, this role-play, and the discussion afterward by the group, opened up a whole new way of thinking about gossip for me. Here's how it went:

> As the scene opens, Janice, the supervisor, is sitting alone at her desk. Her employee, Cynthia, approaches her.
>
> Cynthia is quite agitated as she explains to Janice, "I really need to talk to you about something. I have to ask you," she says in a pleading tone, "please don't tell anyone in the office. My husband just left me, and it was a surprise. I can barely deal with it. I'm barely functioning here," she says, choking back tears. "On top of that," she goes on, with her shoulders and head slowly

drooping forward, "I just got back from the doctor and I have to have a hysterectomy!"

"Oh my goodness," exclaims Janice with a look of concern on her face as she reaches over to pat Cynthia on the arm. "I'm so sorry to hear this."

Cynthia goes on to explain about her need for privacy. "I really need to keep this quiet." She looks Janice in the eyes pleadingly. "I don't want people coming up to me. I can't deal with it emotionally right now. It's just too much. Is that all right?"

"I understand completely," Janice says.

We next see Janice as she enters the lunchroom with a worried frown creasing her forehead. She is trying to maintain her resolve to keep quiet as she approaches two women waiting for her at a table for lunch. "Uhh!" is the sound of her resolve escaping as she loses the battle. "I just had a—you can't say anything!" The two women agree. "Cynthia's having a hard time, and I just want to, you know—this has to be confidential. But we really need to support her and to help her. She's having problems in her marriage, and female problems, too. I can't go into the details. I trust you two to keep this under wraps. I'm just saying something because we just really want to support her."

The two women agree, "Yes, of course!"

After a quick lunch, Janice gets up to leave. After she leaves, one of her lunch partners, Andrea, gets up and goes over to another table with two women having lunch and sits down.

Practically whispering, she asks, "Did you hear about Cynthia?"

"No, what?" they say, leaning in with curiosity, glad to be sharing what is apparently a secret.

"Yeah, she's got some female problems and some marital issues. You have to keep it quiet, though. Don't tell anybody where you heard this from. All right? You know, we just want to be there for her and make sure to support her."

The two women mumble their agreement, and they all get up and go their separate ways. One of them, Sandra, sees Cynthia in the hall and goes over to her. "Oh my gosh, Cynthia, I just heard," says Sandra, as all the color drains from Cynthia's face and her mouth sags open in surprise. "I'm so sorry about everything that's going on! I've had two miscarriages myself, so I know what it's like. And, you know, my husband and I were separated for a time." Cynthia is mortified as it hits her that everyone knows, and she hides her face in her hands. "We were able, through counseling, to work it out, though, so don't give up," says Sandra. "Gotta run!" She hurries off, noticing that her supportive comments have not been well received and feeling a little bit hurt about it.

Cynthia groans. The role-play ends.

As I watched the role-play, I thought, "Yuck! Another role-play about gossip!" But when I asked the group to discuss what they had seen, an argument broke out about whether or not this role-play was about gossip. I was baffled. I could not understand what the argument was about, but the group quickly changed the subject and went on to discuss the other three role-plays that had been performed. I left the session still confused about that argument.

Gossip versus Transknitting

Shortly after the experience of this role-play and discussion, I went to visit my mother and I heard myself ask her, "So, Mom, what have you heard about people I know?" As she told me about an old friend of hers who had cancer and the daughter of another friend who just graduated from medical school, I asked myself, "What are we doing right now? Are we gossiping?" It didn't feel like gossip. Then I remembered that every Saturday morning when I talk to my friend Margaret, our conversations begin with "How's your mother? How's your sister? What happened to your friend's daughter?" I may not even know the friend's daughter—in fact, I may not even know Margaret's friend, but she matters to Margaret, so I ask about her to connect with Margaret.

Reflecting on these conversations helped me realize that as women, we have a range of talk that can be about other people. Some of it is really mean and damaging, and some of it is not. Some of it is about connecting with each other through talking about other people, and some of it is about our intention to be supportive of someone else. Scholars have described these positive intentions behind gossip, and other forms of indirect communication, and the constructive impact these behaviors can have on maintaining community connections.[1] It's about intention, and this was what the argument was about in the research group. The reason for the disagreement was that the intention behind talking about Cynthia was to be supportive of her, and this did not register as gossip for some group members.

Yes, Janice, the supervisor, broke her promise to Cynthia and damaged the trust between them—that was poorly handled by Janice. When she realized that she could not keep her agreement, Janice needed to go back to Cynthia and work out with her how to talk about her situation with others to develop team support to cover her work while she was on medical leave—or else Janice needed to keep her promise not to say anything. We need to be able to trust each other, so we have to behave in ways that build trust.

Upon further reflection, I realized that when I asked the women in my research groups to talk about gossip, there was a lot of messy, muddy confusion in what they said. It seems that we do have a range of talk that can involve other people, but we have only one umbrella term for the whole range of talk—"gossip"—which has a very negative connotation. I decided that we need more language to help us distinguish between the constructive and destructive types of talk about others. I created the term "transknitting" to describe the kinds of talk about others that is about transferring (trans) information for the purpose of connecting (knitting or looping together) to someone or maintaining community or about a positive intention to support someone who might need help.

An example of how transknitting works as a way of connecting occurred one day at home. My partner, Mike, came home from work bewildered. His daughter had heard from his ex-wife that he had been ill and called to inquire about how he was feeling.

The bewildering part was that Mike and his ex-wife, Patty, have been divorced for twenty-five years and have not been on speaking terms during that time.

"How does she know I'm sick?" he demanded to know.

I suggested that the only way his ex-wife could have known he had been ill was that his *other* daughter must have told her.

"Why are they talking about me?" he asked. "Don't I have a say about who talks about me? And besides, why does Patty care whether or not I'm sick after all this time?"

"You don't have a say, she doesn't care, and," I answered, "this isn't about you."

"What do you mean 'it's not about me'?" he said. "I'm the one they're talking about."

"They are transknitting," I replied. "You are not the point. They are using information about you to do their mother-daughter relationship work. This is really not about you."

They were talking about Mike to connect, just as my mother and I talked about people we both knew to connect. There was no negative intention toward Mike. His daughters and their mother were engaging in one of the positive types of talk.

But distinguishing what type of talk about others we are about to do is not always easy in the moment. In fact, we don't usually even think about it. When I made the distinction in language between gossip and transknitting and started talking about it with my friends, our interactions started to change immediately. We would say to each other, "Oh, wait a minute. I was just about to tell you something, but, let me think— is it gossip or transknitting?" We began to be able to hold ourselves accountable for what we were doing, and it made a huge difference. We could make conscious choices not to participate in negative or hurtful types of talk about other people.

It's not that we don't know when we are about to share gossip that has a negative intention, it's just that we don't stop to make a conscious choice about whether or not we really want to do that. Having new language, like "transknitting," can help us make a choice. Without an awareness that transknitting is a positive type of talk, we can feel bad about ourselves as women and bad about women for talking about other people, even when the intent is positive.

Some scholars have identified ways that we can feel bad about ourselves because we believe the negative stereotypes, or internalized distorted images, about our group.[2] The prevalence of such beliefs was why the responses were so muddy and confused when I asked the research participants about gossip. In another example, when I asked the participants in a different group session for a show of hands from those who engage in gossip, no one responded. When I asked about this nonresponse during follow-up individual interviews, participants attached shame and guilt to the concept of gossip, as reflected by Sheri, a technology manager:

> I'm sorry! We all lied! I think gossip by women is very common. It's kind of embarrassing to think that it is this common. You know you shouldn't be talking about people behind their backs. It's just not nice.

Another example of the internalized negative image of women as gossipers was explained by Tara, a white nurse in her thirties who said, "We're catty. We like to get involved in people's lives." The terms "catty" and "catfight" are very negative and are associated only with the behavior of women. They reflect a stereotype of women as backstabbing and untrustworthy. The government managers explained, during their group discussion, how gossip is negatively associated with women more so than with men. One group member explained,

> In so many workplaces, including mine, if four men stand around and talk, they're just men standing around and talking. If four women stand around and talk, they're gossiping. If a man shares information about what's going on with somebody else personally in the workplace, then this is because he is taking a concerned view. But if a woman shares information of a personal nature, then she's catty.

This negative stereotype about women as catty is very widespread in US culture. What we can do to change this perception is distinguish gossip from transknitting and stop gossiping. When we make the choice to engage in transknitting, we can celebrate what's positive about women's talk and feel good about it. Transknitting builds teams, strengthens community, and builds relationships.

Gossip is one type of indirect communication. We will now consider others as well as some cultural differences.

Indirect Communication: Triangulation and Conflict Avoidance

Two types of indirect communication that are common patterns between women in the workplace are triangulation and conflict avoidance. Deborah Tannen, a linguistic scholar who focuses on gender differences in communication styles, reminds us that there is a tendency in the United States to think of indirectness as a female style.[3] She points out that, in fact, most of the world's cultures have indirect styles as the norm for both women and men. For example, in Japan, it is too face-threatening to say no to someone, and so many forms of yes have evolved, some of which mean no. Listeners understand which form of yes they are hearing.

While many women in the United States, and a majority of the women in this study, feel more comfortable with indirect communication, we will review some racial and ethnic differences in this pattern. But first, let's take a look at some patterns described by the study participants about indirect communication between women at work.

Triangulation as a form of indirect communication was a common pattern described by study participants. Marissa, one of the government managers, put it this way:

> There's always sort of triangulated conversations between women. A doesn't talk to B, but A talks to C, expecting C to say something to B, so B will change the way things work with A.

One way of understanding the purpose of triangulation, also found in all indirect cultures, is that it is a passive style of dealing with conflict.[4] When asked how they felt about dealing with conflict, the women in this study, particularly white American and Hispanic women, expressed a discomfort with direct confrontation. Here are some ways they described their discomfort:

- "It's hard for me. I'm not good at confrontation." (Paula, nurse)

- "I don't like confrontation. I allowed a coworker to intimidate me." (Laurie, manager in the travel industry)

- "I'm a wimp! I would let conflict slide and then come around, behind the scenes, and do that passive-aggressive thing. That's not good." (Sheri, technology manager)

- "It's difficult because you don't want to make somebody angry." (Claire, nurse)

Paula summed it up best for this group of women: "We weren't raised that way [to be direct and confrontational]. We were told that women didn't do that...you were to be seen and not heard." "Seen and not heard"—I remember being told this when I was growing up, along with "girls are sugar and spice and everything nice." I remember thinking that I had to avoid confrontation because it could damage a relationship—or, as Claire said, "make somebody angry." But I eventually realized that damage to the relationship was much more likely to occur when I avoided conflict and did not deal directly with differences. By letting bad feelings pile up, I was creating distance and sending mixed messages. When people deal directly with misunderstandings or hurt feelings and clear them up, relationships actually get stronger. Many of us don't have the skills to be direct, but they can be learned. While indirect communication, which is preferred in many cultures, can have a constructive purpose in the workplace, direct communication, such as describing feelings and giving and receiving feedback, helps strengthen and maintain work relationships.

One important cultural difference in the study participants around the issue of conflict avoidance was observed between white American and black American women. Scholars note that because of differences in experience historically, many African American women are not conflict avoidant and value directness.[5] During the time of slavery in the United States, white women were treated as too frail and dainty to undertake physical labor, while black women were treated as beasts of burden and subjected to the same demeaning labor and hardships as black men.[6] Patricia Hill Collins, a black feminist scholar, explains that African American women learned to place a "high value on personal expressiveness" and directness as a survival mechanism.[7] These differences in direct versus indirect confrontation styles can mean that African American women often feel that white American women are dishonest or uninterested in meaningful engagement with them because the white women are reserved and subdued in both what they say and how they say it.[8] The cultures of these two groups have been shaped by very different historical forces; consequently, members of these two groups are particularly vulnerable to misunderstandings with each other.

Relational Resilience and Relational Courage

Relational resilience, a concept developed by Jean Baker Miller and other relational cultural theory (RCT) scholars, is what we need to develop to be able to deal with conflict directly and recover from the misunderstandings that can occur because of our differences and disappointments.[9] In fact, Miller explains that we grow most deeply as individuals and in relationships when we encounter difference and work through it.[10] To learn to stay engaged in the face of conflict (rather than withdrawing or disappearing) is a skill that strengthens relationships. Staying engaged, or having relational resilience, even when you are really hurt, mad, or disappointed in another woman, requires something called "relational courage," where, even though you may feel fear or discomfort about directly confronting someone, you are able to face the discomfort or fear and have the conversation instead of withdrawing from the relationship.[11] Here is a story of how relational courage worked to save a friendship.

Two women friends, Molly and Julie, came to me for help because after years of being close colleagues and personal friends, a misunderstanding had occurred and they were both deeply hurt by the behaviors of the other during a series of events. They had tried to talk about it themselves, but they were not able to make progress and were feeling quite stuck. They reached out for help with the hope of being able to stay friends, but a lot of distance had developed between them by the time they called me. They both reported feeling fearful of attending the session because what they might say or hear could create additional injury and because the session might fail to save the relationship and they would have to face the fact that it was over. It took relational courage for both of them to even show up.

I proposed a structure and process for the session, a tool that is described in detail in the next section of this chapter that allowed each woman to listen really deeply to the other, to feel heard by the other, and to acknowledge her part in creating the other's hurt. Each person learned something new about the impact of her behavior on the other. Each had a chance to say "I get it. I'm sorry" in her own way and in her own time. We were able to create something that RCT scholars call "mutual empathy."[12] It worked to heal the relationship.

Women often don't take such positive steps. Instead we cut off the other person and never tell her what happened, or we triangulate with someone else, hoping word will get back to the person that we are upset. And cultural differences can make it even more difficult to spend time with each other and really understand how the other person sees things. But we can learn to do this, and we can salvage important relationships and strengthen them.

A Tool for Repairing Relationships by Creating Mutual Empathy

The goal of the two-hour facilitated session with Molly and Julie was to create mutual empathy because they were stuck and unable to make progress in repairing their relationship. In fact, it seemed that the relationship might be over, and engaging a third party for support was a last-ditch effort by these two friends. Judith Jordan notes that for relationship change to occur an injured person needs for the offending party to hear about her experience. She needs to feel responded to with interest and concern.[13] As we have also discussed, many of the expectations we have of each other are unconscious or unstated. Furthermore, we can sometimes ascribe intentions to the behaviors of another person, based on our past experiences that have nothing to do with what the other person is thinking. For all these reasons, it was important to create a setting where each woman had the opportunity to listen deeply to the other, to feel heard by the other, and to acknowledge her part in the other's experience. (See table 5 for a summary of the process.)

The process used with Molly and Julie is described below.

Step 1: Presession interviews

The facilitator conducts a presession interview by phone, before the face-to-face session. Each party is asked to state her hopes for the meeting and to describe what a positive outcome would be. She then tells her version of what happened and why she felt hurt. The purpose of the interview is to help each woman organize her thoughts and her story, to allow the facilitator to know key details of her story to remind her of them during the session if she forgot something significant, and to build the rapport between each woman and the facilitator.

Step 2: The Two-Hour Face-to-Face Session

The parties arrange a two-hour meeting in a quiet, neutral location.

The Facilitator Role

The role of the third party, or facilitator, for the face-to-face session is to propose a structure, to get buy-in from the participants to the structure, to help both parties listen to each other and not interrupt each other, and to ensure that both feel heard. The facilitator may help keep track of time boundaries that the parties agree to. Time boundaries may be open ("take all the time you need") or fixed ("take 20 minutes each"), based upon the structure that is agreed upon. It can be helpful, at the beginning of the session, for the facilitator to express her belief that this process can really work and has worked with others to invite an open mind set for the participants.

Roles and Process for Speaker and Listener

Each woman takes turns being either the speaker or the listener. This means that the person who goes first as the speaker has all the time she needs, or all the agreed-upon time, to tell her version of the story, as she perceives it, of how she was hurt and why. During this time, the listener can ask clarifying questions or check for understanding (sparingly), but she cannot argue, debate, express her own opinions, or tell her story.

Once the speaker has finished, the listener summarizes what she heard and the speaker corrects that understanding until she feels heard by the listener. The listener doesn't have to agree; she just has to demonstrate that she heard the speaker's perspective.

Once the speaker verifies that she feels heard, then the listener can state what she heard that was a new insight or new information to her. She will have more opportunity to do this again at the end of the session. The listener may be able to apologize at this point by saying something like, "I'm sorry that my actions/behaviors caused this hurt for you." If she is not ready to apologize, this can come at the end, but the sooner it can be done, and the more often it can be done, the better!

Role Reversal

Next, the listener and speaker switch roles and repeat the process described above for speaker and listener.

Wrap-Up

Next, each party states or repeats what she heard from the other party that was a new insight or a deeper understanding. Each apologizes for what she said or did that caused hurt for the other person. (Note: Her intentions are irrelevant. What is important is to acknowledge the impact of her behavior.)

For the next step in the process, the facilitator asks each party to make a statement about how she is feeling at the end of this session. Usually, if the participants have fully engaged in the process and have been open, they will say that they are hopeful or cautiously optimistic, reflecting the development of some mutual empathy that has reopened their connection and made renewal of the friendship possible. Because this is a deeply emotional process for most people, it can be hard for people to fully articulate their understandings and feelings, and the facilitator can help people feel comfortable to express themselves.

As a final contribution, the facilitator again expresses her belief that this process can really work and has worked with others. She can encourage the parties to stay hopeful and be open to moving forward together and letting go of the past.

TABLE 5. Guidelines for creating relational resilience

Goal: To create mutual empathy to repair a relationship

Skills and Competencies Needed: Listening skills, skills for asking clarifying questions, the ability to apologize.

Process: Turn taking as both speaker and listener

Before the face-to-face meeting

- The participants engage support from a third party to facilitate the meeting.
- The facilitator interviews each woman before a two-hour face-to-face meeting.

During the two-hour face-to-face meeting

- The speaker tells her story until she feels she has conveyed the important points.
- The listener summarizes what she understood until the speaker feels fully heard.
- The listener shares new insights or understandings gained from listening to the speaker.
- The listener apologizes for the impact of her actions, if she is ready.
- The participants switch roles and repeat the above steps.
- In the wrap-up, each participant repeats what she now understands and apologizes again.
- Each participant shares a feeling about the session (hopeful, optimistic, etc.).

NEXT STEPS

The following exercises are designed to help you strengthen your relationship skills and become more trustworthy.

1. Practice your listening skills.

   a. Listen to someone else without interrupting for five minutes while she talks about something she cares about that she is either dealing with or is frustrated by. You can use nonverbal behaviors, such as nodding or raising your eyebrows, to show that you are listening, but you cannot say anything. Notice what gets in the way of fully listening, and bring your attention back to the speaker. Notice how quickly you may want to interrupt and interject your opinions or your own experiences—but don't interrupt.

b. Now it's your turn. Ask the listener to let you talk for five minutes about something you care about that you are dealing with or are frustrated by. Notice your reaction to having five minutes to talk without interruption. Is this situation unusual? Do you like it? Do you dislike it? Just notice.

2. Distinguish gossip from transknitting. Share the definition of "transknitting" with two other women, one at work and one outside of work whom you talk with regularly. During your conversations, when discussing another person, ask each other, "Is this gossip or transknitting? What do you think?"

3. If you have a relationship that has recently become strained or has come to an end for reasons that you may or may not understand, consider asking for help with using the relational resilience tool described above.

5

Behind the Door and under the Bus: Intentionally Hurtful Behaviors

Why does it happen?

Sabotage by women colleagues—it happens for a reason. It is *not*, as many women in my research said, "just the way women are." Nonetheless, it happens, is very painful, and happens way too often. In 2011, the American Management Association conducted a survey of one thousand working women and found that 95 percent of them believed they were undermined by another woman at some point in their careers.[1] This topic is always of urgent interest to many in the audiences to whom I speak and in my workshops. They want to know how to deal with it. In this chapter, we will consider why sabotage and other hurtful behaviors happen in the workplace between women. In the next chapter, we will explore options for what to do about it on both the organizational and interpersonal levels.

Am I Still in the Middle School Lunchroom?

We must understand why hurtful behaviors happen with such high frequency between women at work before taking a look at ways to prevent and stop these behaviors. Understanding why they happen will help us consider a broader range of strategies for change and help us stop assuming that this is about some quality that most women are born with. First, we need to take a closer look at two concepts: (1) internalized negative stereotypes and (2) societal and workplace structures that set us up against each other, starting in childhood in the middle school lunchroom, if not earlier.

Internalized Negative Stereotypes

In chapter 4, we stated that the term "gossip" has a very negative connotation and is associated with women more so than with men, even though men also talk about other people. We also noted that the women who participated in this research reflected an internalization of this negative stereotype about women by expressing guilt and shame about the prevalence of gossip.

When we feel bad about ourselves and other members of our group—women, in this case—we have internalized, or come to believe, the negative stereotypes about women. When we internalize the negative messages about women, we are more vulnerable to being hurt by another woman. For example, when, as a young woman, I was on vacation with a group of women, a woman in our group said to me, with a bit of a sarcastic tone in her voice (as I heard it), "I think it's great that you are so comfortable with your body." Until that time, I had always loved sunbathing in a bikini for maximum tanning exposure. But I interpreted her comment to mean that I did not measure up to acceptable societal standards of female beauty—I was not thin or blond. I immediately felt shame about my body, and I never wore a bikini again. So we can hurt ourselves or feel bad about ourselves when someone makes a comment that triggers internalized societal messages about how women are supposed to be that do not match how we are or the choices we've made, such as "women's place is in the home, not the workplace." We can feel that we do not deserve the credit for our accomplishments (called the "imposter phenomenon") or that something is wrong with us in other ways.[2]

Internalization of negative stereotypes about women was reflected in the words the research participants used in making general statements about women such as "catty," "backbiting," and "catfights." Karen, one of the white nurses in her twenties in the research, gave an example of this stereotyping when she said,

> There is always a gossip factor with nurses. It is actually an inside joke to nurses throughout the country that we say, "Oh, well, you know it is all women here. This is how it is—catty and gossipy," and it is said frequently. Actually, it's unfortunate because not all women are like that, but people will say, "You know how women are."

These statements reflect a stereotype of women as backstabbing and untrustworthy, and one thing we can all do is stop using this language to describe women.

Scholars across disciplines have described a number of ways in which our behaviors as women can be influenced by the phenomenon of internalizing negative stereotypes about women. Paolo Freire explains that it is common for members of marginalized groups to strike out at members of their own groups. He calls this behavior "horizontal violence," defined as oppressed group members "striking out at their own comrades for the pettiest reasons" as the result of internalizing the negative messages about them in the larger society.[3] Hurtful gossip and other intentionally hurtful behaviors are typical oppressed-group behaviors used by marginalized group members to keep one another in line or to feel more powerful in the face of feeling devalued by the power group (in this case, white men).[4] Regardless of how horizontal violence is described, it includes a survival component that involves competition for scarce resources and for acceptance from the dominant group.

Another example of behavior that reflects horizontal violence between women is the phenomenon, referenced in earlier chapters, of women being harsher on other women than men are. A 2008 study of nearly eighteen hundred employees by the University of Toronto found that women working under female supervisors reported more symptoms of physical and psychological stress than those working under male supervisors.[5] Remember the frequency of study participants reporting that they would rather work for a man than a woman?

We are not talking only about gossip and harsher treatment from women bosses, though. Scholars describe a continuum of aggression that hurts people and can damage careers. But let's be clear—*all* oppressed or marginalized groups act out the internalized negative messages about their groups by engaging in these same types of hurtful behaviors. This is not just about women. This is not "just the way women are."

Deep Patterns from the Middle School Lunchroom

I began to wonder about the connection between the "mean girl" literature on adolescent girls and the frequency of undermining behavior reported between adult women in the workplace. A number of the women who participated in my research also mentioned the similarity of the negative dynamics between women in the workplace and the types of "mean girl" behaviors described for adolescent girls. Keri, a white nurse in her forties, explained,

> I expect them in adolescence. I don't expect them at forty-five or fifty. Oh, I'm certain that the bullies in junior high school are still bullies today. Have you been to a high school reunion?

Although these behaviors are frequently said to be related, few studies have been conducted to make a direct connection between adolescent "mean girl" behavior and adult women's experiences with each other in the workplace. Yet the connection seems obvious and could explain why the negative experiences of women with each other in the workplace are so pervasive. These behaviors probably reflect marginalized group behavior that is ancient, deeply held, and learned at a very young age.

A frequent question from my audiences is, "But aren't things different now for girls than they used to be, with Title IX and access to sports?" While some situations have surely changed, and change is always happening, two excellent studies conducted in 2002 and 2003 that covered diverse groups of girls from first grade to high school in various parts of the country found that the messages adolescent girls still receive have not changed in significant ways.[6] Girls still learn from the larger culture that how they look (being skinny and blond) is more important than how smart or talented they are—and so many girls, including girls of color, have no hope of ever measuring up to the cultural standard. There is still a widespread expectation among girls that they will subordinate their own dreams and goals to please a man when they grow up and that they will be the primary caregivers in their families. Check out the magazines and websites that adolescent girls read to find these types of messages. Girls may now expect to work once they are parents, but they still may not expect to be the primary breadwinner unless they have grown up in a single-parent household.

Girls also notice that there are very few girls in action roles in their preschool and elementary school books. In those books, most girls still sit on the sidelines, while boys have the adventures and rescue them. Or the girls notice that the witches are almost always female. I recently went to a well-known children's bookstore to buy books for a friend's newborn daughter. I wanted to find young children's books that showed girls in leadership roles, and it was excruciatingly difficult to find any. Most of the characters were boys, even the animal characters. The societal messages to young children that it is better or more fun to be a boy and that how a girl looks is all that matters are still quite strong.

Scholars suggest that we must understand that "mean girl" behavior, also described as indirect aggression and relational aggression, happens in the context of a patriarchal system that values boys more than girls and limits the behavioral options for girls.[7] Girls feel powerless when they are told they must be orderly and nice. Boys are allowed to be rowdy and get called upon by the teacher without raising their hands, while girls have to follow the rules. And girls feel pressure to gain the approval of adults by meeting their gendered expectations. While the studies show some differences by class and race about what these expectations are, there is consistency in the limited avenues open to girls to feel powerful without being labeled "deviant." Researchers point out that every child wants three things out of life: connection, recognition, and power.[8] Girls' power is diminished by societal injunctions to be passive bystanders: they must hide their "not nice" feelings of anger, they must soften and silence their voices, and they still need the attention of boys to have self-worth.[9]

Scholars note that to feel powerful, girls become active participants in horizontal violence, which Paolo Freire says is a manifestation of oppression or restriction.[10] Researchers of adolescent girls explain that "girls' meanness to other girls is a result of their struggle to make sense of or to reject their secondary status in the world and to find ways to have power."[11]

One of the rules for how to be nice and nonthreatening is to not show anger. Girls are expected to be "sweet, caring, precious, and tender" and to have "no bad thoughts or feelings."[12] So while boys can vent their anger outwardly, girls cannot. If boys show strong feelings, they are called "assertive" and "competitive," while girls who do the same are called "bossy" and "confrontational." Rachel Simmons, in her study of girls in ten different schools, diverse by race, social class, and geography, points out that girls don't feel angry in fundamentally different ways than boys, but many girls show anger differently because they have learned they must do so to gain the approval of adults.[13] Girls learn to "fly under the radar" of adults by expressing their natural feelings of aggression indirectly and subtly, while keeping up the appearance of being nice.

Simmons found a hidden culture of girls' aggression in which bullying is epidemic, distinctive, and destructive. Because open conflict is not acceptable behavior for girls, girls fight with body language and relationships instead of fists and knives. Friendship is a weapon, and anger is rarely articulated.[14] Various researchers note that alternative aggression starts in preschool, and so do the first signs of sex differences. In the middle school years, a second socialization begins that sets a template in place for adult behavior.[15] In middle school and earlier, girls are very conscious of the swirling underbelly of alternative aggression, and their part in it, as they try to figure out the rules for relational success. Have a conversation with any girl between the ages of nine and thirteen, and she will tell you all about it in great detail. By high school, scholars agree, girls have learned to take indirect aggression for granted.[16] By adulthood, women are more likely to become unconscious of their own participation in alternative aggression.

Indirect aggression is a strategy used by those with less power because those with more power either cannot detect the aggressive act or don't know whom to punish. This is a particularly useful strategy for girls because it provides a cover for unfeminine emotions like anger.[17] Girls can feel powerful by being mean without being accountable either to other girls or to adult authority figures.

Two scholars, Terri Apter and Ruthellen Josselson, also noted the similarity of adolescent-girl behaviors with the patterns described in their interviews with adult women.[18] Many of these women described their workplaces as having much in common with junior high, such as subgroups and shifting alliances with female coworkers, where issues of loyalty and betrayal become the emotional center of the workday. Even as grown-up women, we carry our adolescent selves around with us.

We have now considered that sabotage and other hurtful behaviors between women in the workplace happen for a reason. These behaviors are, in fact, ones that all marginalized groups exhibit. It is well documented that women are still a marginalized group in the workplace, with significant differences by class, race, and nationality within the larger group in access to opportunity and higher pay.

We have also seen that these behaviors exhibited by adult women in the workplace actually begin in childhood for the same reasons—as a response to feeling less powerful as girls. We come to adulthood with these deeply learned patterns of behavior toward others of our marginalized group and enter a workplace context that continues to devalue feminine norms of behavior (see chapter 1) and that has limited spaces for women at the top (see chapter 2). It is no surprise that horizontal violence is alive and well between adult women in the workplace, where the limited spaces at the top set us up to see each other as competition, and those old childhood patterns of lashing out at each other when we feel devalued can be easily triggered. A recent article in the *Wall Street Journal* about women leaders explained, "In a world where there are still relatively few women in positions of power—just

3% of Fortune 500 CEOs—it is an understandable assumption that the rise of one would mean the ouster of another. One for one, instead of one plus one."[19]

Let's now take a look at the types of negative behavior described by the participants in this research.

Two Types of Aggression

The fact that all marginalized groups engage in horizontal violence doesn't make the experience of being undermined by another woman any less hurtful or damaging. I asked the women who participated in this research to describe any experiences they had of feeling undermined or sabotaged at work by another woman. Their responses revealed a continuum of behaviors that correspond to the ways that horizontal violence is expressed. This continuum of behaviors falls within a range from "indirect aggression" on the milder end to "career aggression" on the severe end.

Indirect Aggression

Indirect aggression is behavior that is purposefully hurtful and also denied. It is very similar to the alternative aggression described by scholars for adolescent girls.[20] Here is one of many examples of indirect aggression provided by a nurse, Keri, in the study:

> I walked in and there were two of the women that were in my group walking ahead of me. I said, "Oh, hey—how are you guys?" And they kind of looked over their shoulder and gave me this look, with that curl in their lip and roll in their eyes. They got on the elevator and as the doors closed, one of them said, "We're going to get coffee"—click—and the door closed in my face.

As seen above, indirect aggression includes both verbal and nonverbal covert behaviors that could seem innocuous but are intended to hurt. They can include not only the use of body language, such as eye rolling, but also silence, as demonstrated in the story from another white nurse in her fifties, Janet, about her interactions with other women at work:

I'd go up to talk with them about something, and they'd all pick up the phone and pretend they were talking. So, for the longest time, I thought, "God, they're on the phone a lot!" You know, it was just a smoke and mirrors kind of thing—and I was brand new to the organization, a lot younger than them, and they certainly weren't going to let me in.

Smoke and mirrors—now add to this another thread in indirect aggression—denial. One example of denial in the adolescent-girl literature includes this description by a ninth grader: "Last week, I asked my friend why she was mad at me—I had no idea why—and she said, 'I'm not mad at you.' Right then I knew she was mad at me."[21]

Another young girl in this same study explained the payoff of denial for both adolescents and adults: "If you don't tell someone why you're mad, you can't get a rebuttal. You win."[22]

An adult participant in this study, Laurie, who works in the travel industry, shared an example of denial by a woman colleague, Debbie, involving Debbie's recommendation to her boss, David, that the position of another colleague, Brian, be eliminated. Brian found out from David that, based on Debbie's proposal, he would soon be losing his job. When Brian confronted Debbie, she said, "I don't know what you're talking about. David and I haven't spoken."

In exasperation, Laurie explained, "It was just a flat-out lie. It was a lie that she clearly got caught in and even to Brian's face she would not admit it." Debbie's denial qualifies as indirect aggression because she knew she had intentionally done something that would have negative consequences for Brian yet denied it to his face.

Kate, a manager in the financial services industry, described another type of indirect aggression. She told me about receiving a negative performance review, which was a complete surprise to her—not from her woman boss but from her boss's boss:

> January was when I started my new role. Probably three months later, my old boss scheduled a yearly performance review with me, which was unusual for a lot of reasons. Normally,

performance reviews are more timely. And she had her boss on the phone with her. She doesn't like confrontation, so I felt like she was having him do it for her. She didn't say a word the whole time. It was like she was just sitting in the background, listening.

I was just shocked to get a negative performance review, even though on paper my numbers looked good. It felt like a lot of things had transpired behind the scenes so that she could throw Kate under the bus.

For Kate, the indirect aggression happened when her boss threw Kate under the bus by undermining her behind the scenes and then having someone else deliver the bad news.

One more example of behavior that is intended to be hurtful but is denied, using silence as a weapon, was demonstrated in one of the role-plays developed by research participants who were managers in state government. The aggression was indirect but quite mean in its intentions:

Four women who work together in an office have just come back from lunch. Marcia was not included in the outing.

"I'm stuffed," declares Lee, puffing out her cheeks and dropping a container of leftover food on her desk.

"That was a good place to go," notes Judy, suggesting that they go back again sometime.

Rose casually asks, seemingly to no one in particular, as she takes off her coat, "Do you want to go out after work today?"

Lee says yes and suggests, "Do you want to go to that place that we went last Friday?" Judy, Rose, and Arleen agree that this was a cool place and they would like to go there after work.

In the meantime, Marcia has been sitting at her desk in the same work area, listening to this postlunch chatter and wondering what she has to do to be included in this group. The women seem to have such a good time, and she wishes they would give her a chance to show she could fit in with them. She decides to take a shot at it. Maybe she hasn't been assertive enough and they think she isn't interested. She sees an opening in the conversation and says, "Do you know where one of my favorite places is?"

She is chagrined when they ignore her and continue chatting as though she hasn't spoken and isn't there.

"So let's plan on going to that same place," says Lee, turning her back to Marcia, rolling her eyes, and giving a knowing look at Rose and Arleen.

"We'll be there—what time do you guys want to get there?"

"How about seven?" offers Arleen. "We can take my car. I've got enough room for four," she says, making it clear that no one else is going to join their group.

Marcia screws up her courage and decides to give it one more try, figuring she has nothing to lose, and asks, "Did you know there's a new club that's actually got a place for the kids?" No one responds to her this time, either.

After a short, pregnant pause, Lee declares, "All right! Break's over!" The role-play ends.

Welcome to the middle school lunchroom in the grown-up workplace. While this was a role-play, it was presented as an example of typical dynamics between women in the workplace. It was one of many such role-plays presented during the study to demonstrate indirect aggression— probably an old and deeply buried pattern that is a form of horizontal violence.

Let's now take a look at behaviors that move farther toward the extremely negative end of the continuum.

Career Aggression

Career aggression is behavior that includes indirect aggression but moves beyond hurtful behaviors to actions intended to damage or sabotage the careers of other women (see table 6).

Some of the examples in the previous section on indirect aggression had the potential to damage careers, but the cases that follow show an intent to do career damage that is unmistakable. The parallel concept in the adolescent-girl literature is "social aggression," where the intention is to undermine a girl's credibility and reputation with others.[23] Half the women interviewed for this research reported experiencing career

TABLE 6. Characteristics of indirect and career aggression

Indirect aggression	Career Aggression

• Consists of purposefully hurtful behaviors that are denied when the aggressor is confronted
 	
• Includes verbal and nonverbal covert behaviors, including
 	
  – Eye-rolling
 	
  – Subtle comments, such as "I see you didn't take your smart pill today."
 	
  – Silence as a weapon
 	
  – Spreading negative rumors
	• Includes indirect behaviors but moves beyond them to actions intended to damage or sabotage the career of another woman
	
	• May be perpetrated by a friend, an acquaintance, or a complete stranger in the workplace

aggression from a woman at work, sometimes by a woman they knew and sometimes by someone they weren't acquainted with at all.

Before I share examples of career aggression, I want to acknowledge my concerns as a feminist about reinforcing the worst negative stereotypes about women. Let me reiterate that women can and do have solid, stable, and supportive relationships with other women colleagues, which was often stressed by the women in this research. It is also true that men sabotage each other's careers. The significance here for women is that in the midst of all the challenges we encounter in organizations because of gender biases and other structural problems previously discussed, we add to the headwinds we face and participate in our own oppression by undermining each other when the opposite behavior is needed to change our situation. Only by acknowledging this problem can we begin to understand and change our behavior so that we can trust each other and work together to change our organizations for the good of all.

Because half the women in this study reported experiences of career aggression by a woman colleague, which is comparable with other studies, this is not an insignificant pattern and it needs to be brought out into the light of day for honest appraisal, negotiation between women, and systemic changes.[24] It will serve us to look honestly at these behaviors and understand them as horizontal violence that happens for a reason. We must take steps, described in the next chapter, to stop career aggression not only because of the obvious harm to careers that can result but because of the long-term psychological and emotional damage that can result for individuals.[25] Such experiences can result in a loss of confidence and self-esteem, as well as a loss of ability to trust others, whether the career aggression is related to sexism, racism, homophobia, xenophobia, class prejudice, or some combination of attacks on the dimensions of a person's identity. The pain created by these acts drains energy from individuals and organizations.[26] We can change these patterns with consciousness, intention, and joint action. We will explore some ways to change this dynamic in chapter 6, but for now, let's get clearer about the differences between indirect aggression and career aggression.

Tammy, who works in the travel industry, starts us off with a story of organizational embarrassment that she described as career sabotage:

> A new woman had started at the company, and I had been with the company for about two years. I had a very strong relationship with my boss and his boss, and we had been working together for a while. This new woman came in and felt threatened, I think, by the relationship that I had with my bosses and the team and probably with my peers as well. She falsely reported me to HR for having a romantic relationship with one of the bosses. I'd define that as sabotage.

This story is an example of career sabotage, as opposed to simply indirect aggression, because the intention seemed to be to damage Tammy's standing in the organization. Tammy described hearing at the "water cooler" that someone was circulating rumors about her. But she was surprised and very embarrassed to be called by the Human Resources Department (HR) and asked very probing questions about her personal life based on rumors started by a person as yet unidentified to Tammy. The tactics of the HR representatives indicated to Tammy that they believed the rumors and that her credibility had been damaged. While Tammy eventually found out who had circulated the rumors, she did not know the woman involved. In the absence of any type of relationship between Tammy and her saboteur, this story of career aggression represents a clear example of horizontal violence—oppressed group members taking their frustration out on other members of their group, in this case woman to woman. It couldn't have been a personal vendetta when Tammy didn't even know the other woman.

In the next example, Kendra, a white manager in her fifties in a consulting firm, described taking a new job and experiencing career aggression:

> This group of three women who had been there a long time, who were all friends, began to really try to sabotage me. They'd give me hate mail in my in-box. This was before e-mail. They would steal my mail and throw it away. They would put a key to the side of my car on both sides. They would talk about me incessantly to other people and say I wasn't really very good. They would gossip about me to anybody and they'd tell stories about me, like I was sleeping with the boss, which wasn't true, and they would just try to sabotage me.

Kendra reported that she did not even know who was doing these things to her until considerable time had elapsed. The hate mail and property damage were upsetting, but stealing and destroying her mail had a negative impact on her ability to perform her job when she did not receive information or documents that others thought she had. Her reputation and credibility were also impugned. Once again, Kendra did not know these women.

The key to this dynamic is in Kendra's statement that the women "had been there a long time." She went on to explain that she eventually learned that they did not feel valued and had not been promoted and that she had been hired in above them, even though they were more experienced and had equivalent levels of education—another setup for horizontal violence to be triggered.

The next example of career aggression shows friends turning on a friend to keep her from being hired into a new position. Keri, a nurse, told this story:

> When I worked in the emergency department, I was in charge every night—and the people who worked with me enjoyed me being in charge, or at least that was what was said to me. I had beautiful reviews and had some great pals, many of whom were at my wedding.
>
> Fast-forward about five years, and I have now decided to leave my management position to go back to the emergency department. So I talked to the emergency department manager, who has been a friend of mine for twenty-five years. About three weeks into the process, when I hadn't heard anything, I went back to my friend who was the manager of the emergency department and said, "So what's going on?" She got this really awful look on her face and she twitched—and she was tripping all over herself and said, "You'd better talk to your boss." So I sit down with my boss, who says to me, "There is a problem. They don't want you there." You could have knocked me over with a feather. She went on to say this one, this one, and this one—my friends, people who had been at my wedding—had gone to their bosses and said, "We don't want her."
>
> I was shocked. We would go out after work together; we would talk to each other on days off. Sometimes I would help them out with babysitting or they would help me. If I had any kind of a party or get-together, they were first on my list to invite. They were the people I laughed with at work; they were the people I cried with at work. They were there through my divorce, through a terribly tough time in my life. Why would my friends turn on me like that? That they would stab a friend in the back for no apparent reason for their own selfish gain? Well the bottom line was, they were afraid that I was going to usurp their perceived position.

Keri's story is an example of the impact of mixing friendship expectations with the hierarchical norms of masculine work environments, which can trigger horizontal violence. In such cases, acts of covert career aggression can leave the recipient feeling not only bewildered but shocked when it happens. Career aggression can also damage a woman's self-confidence. Angella, a diplomatic services manager in Mexico, explained that "When someone is saying bad things about you, after a while you start to feel that maybe the bad things are true."

The last, and potentially most damaging, example of career aggression comes from Karen, a nurse in a hospital, who didn't know her aggressor at all:

> She had told people that I had used my own urine in the urine collection for a patient, which never happened. It had no truth to it. It would never happen. I remember just shaking and thinking, "What do I do?" If that had gone to court or something had happened, I would have lost my nursing license.

Career aggression was reported as a common pattern not only by the women who participated in the research in the United States, but also by the women in the other participating countries—Spain, Mexico, China, and India. While in some cases the perpetrators were strangers, in others they were friends—sometimes close friends. By naming these negative patterns, it is my intention as a feminist researcher to illuminate pathways to changing them. To keep things in perspective, however, Keri offers this closing thought, echoed by a majority of the women in this study (and me, too):

> Why does this come as a shock to us? I think when someone who is perceived as a friend or an ally or a compatriot turns on us, it is particularly surprising and painful. But I hate to overplay the mean aspect of women because I, honest to God, have some just wonderful women friends—my soul is rich with women.

NEXT STEPS

Negative stereotypes about women are everywhere, and when we internalize them, we usually do not realize it. Yet carrying these internalized stereotypes can influence our behaviors toward other women. For that reason, it is important to begin to notice how these negative stereotypes may live in us and be reflected in our thoughts, attitudes, and behaviors.

1. The level I statements below describe ways you may be hurting yourself by internalizing negative stereotypes, and the Level II statements describe ways you may be participating in horizontal violence toward another woman.

   Be honest with yourself and put a check mark by the statements below that are true for you. Notice whether your score indicates a low, moderate, or strong internalization of negative stereotypes about women.

Level I—Have you ever

☐ Discounted or doubted yourself?

☐ Apologized before presenting your ideas in a group or meeting, such as saying, "I may be wrong" or "This is probably a stupid question"?

☐ Felt like an imposter or fraud when you got a promotion or opportunity?

☐ Looked in the mirror and really disliked what you saw?

☐ Tied your self-image to your appearance or clothes?

Level II—Have you ever

☐ Said something negative about another woman and denied it when she asked?

☐ Talked negatively about a woman behind her back and smiled to her face?

   ☐ Made a commitment to support another woman and didn't do it when the time came?

   ☐ Said to someone, "She's such a bitch"?

   ☐ Made fun of another woman's appearance behind her back?

   ☐ Said or thought, "You can't trust women"?

   ☐ Spread a rumor that you had heard that cast doubt on another woman's competence?

   ☐ Seen another woman's ideas attacked or ignored in a meeting, whether you agreed with them or not, while you sat back and watched in silence?

Use the following scoring guide to reflect upon your answers:

1–3 checks = You exhibit low internalization of negative stereotypes about women.

4–6 checks = You exhibit moderate internalization of negative stereotypes about women.

7+ checks = You exhibit strong internalization of negative stereotypes about women.

2. Think about your vision for how you would like women to behave toward each other at work. Create a personal code of conduct for how you want to behave. Post it and look at it daily to remind yourself of how you want to be.

6

It's Not "Just the Way Women Are": We Can Change the Patterns

What can we do?

We have established in the previous chapters that the patterns of behavior we have learned are deeply buried in our unconscious, and negative societal messages and organizational structures set us up against each other and can trigger horizontal violence or acts of aggression. But we can change these hurtful and harmful patterns of behavior if we tackle both the organizational and the interpersonal patterns that result in horizontal violence. But we have to attack both levels—organizational and interpersonal—or nothing will change.

Illusions of Powerlessness

One of the first steps we can take is to become aware that feeling powerless is a common experience of marginalized or oppressed groups. This is important because as long as we feel we can do nothing to change the dynamics between women or to change organizational structures and cultures because "it's just the way women are" or "it's just the way things are in organizations," the harmful patterns of behavior will continue.

In almost every case, the women in this research seemed to hold individual women responsible for the difficulties in their relationships or for the negative patterns of behavior they described, either because of "personality problems" or because they said "It's just the way women are." They could not see any other possibility. They seemed unaware that the other women might be acting out internalized stereotypes, even as they themselves held these same stereotypes and blamed "other" women—and not themselves—for acting as "all" women do. They did not see the way systemic forces were setting women up to engage in horizontal violence against each other. We must be able to see these larger forces at play to resist being affected by them and strengthen our ability to support each other. For these reasons, let's turn first to what we can do on the organizational level to prevent the continuum of horizontal violence from happening between women in the workplace.

Organizational Interventions

Powerful forces are at play that influence our internalizing negative beliefs about women. Yet acting out these beliefs against other women is hurtful. Indirect and career aggression are not unconscious acts. However, without an awareness of the systemic forces that provoke these behaviors, and without the skills to name and negotiate our friendship rules and our role boundaries with each other to change what we are doing, we will continue these patterns, deeply rooted in childhood and adolescence.

All-Woman Workshops and Retreats: Awareness, Shared Vision, and Code of Conduct

Because these forces are systemic and the patterns deeply rooted, women need to work in collective settings such as all-woman workshops or retreats to develop a supportive community and to learn to see the systemic forces so they can collectively reject the old patterns, develop a shared vision for the future, and develop new skills together. Choices come from awareness of where our patterns originated—we can then decide what we want to keep and what we want to change about our relationships and our organizations.

Bringing in outside speakers to the all-woman workshops or retreats, sharing reading material on women's dynamics, and creating women's discussion groups to better understand the presentations and readings will help create a shared understanding about why horizontal violence happens. It's not that men won't also benefit from similar learning opportunities, but interrupting the old patterns of horizontal violence needs to begin with women understanding why such aggression happens and working together to stop it. Men can be brought into the learning environment at a later date and benefit from similar learning opportunities both in mixed-gender groups and in all-men settings.

Once we have an awareness of where our patterns come from, groups of women can create a shared vision about the patterns of behavior they would like to see enacted in the future. Creating this shared vision is an important step in rejecting the old patterns and coming to believe that they can stop those old behaviors.

Once the first draft of the new vision is created, the group needs to develop a code of conduct that describes observable behaviors that will bring the vision statement to life. The more widely shared the vision and code of conduct are, the stronger the sense of belonging to a supportive community will be, which is associated with decreased stress and depression and increased energy for change.[1] This sense of belonging will encourage joint effort to use the new behaviors, stop the old patterns of horizontal violence, and work together to create a more inclusive organizational culture.

I have seen the almost immediate impact of raising awareness and developing a shared vision and a code of conduct in many different all-woman client groups. These groups have included boards of trustees, work teams, and long-term leadership development programs. As soon as groups develop their vision statement and code of conduct, behaviors start to change. Because the old patterns of behavior are ancient and deeply held, old behaviors will naturally pop out from time to time, but a shared language and vision will make it easier to call each other on these behaviors and help each other change.

Table 7 is a composite of the vision statements and codes of conduct that groups have created after developing an awareness about the sources of women's dynamics in the workplace.

If your organization does not have the support structures in place to organize workshops and retreats, you can be a catalyst and gather your own network to meet for a monthly lunch or dinner. At these gatherings, you can talk about your vision and create your own code of conduct. You can also invite a group of woman coworkers to your house, have a book discussion, and agree on one action to take together to improve the organization for women.

After groups develop these shared visions and codes of conduct, immediate shifts in behavior that encourage more open and honest communication, improved teamwork, and increased trust can occur. But wanting to behave in these new ways and having the skills to do so are often two different things. For that reason, skill building needs to be the next step on the path to improving our dynamics.

Development of Feedback Skills for Direct Communication

In chapter 4, we observed that indirect or triangulated communication is often a passive style of dealing with conflict. We also considered ways that passively dealing with conflict, or avoiding conflict altogether, while unresolved feelings build up inside can eventually result in damaged relationships. We concluded that when we deal directly with misunderstandings or hurt feelings and clear them up, relationships actually get stronger. Judith Jordan notes that Jean Baker Miller, one of the pioneers of studies on women, says that "good conflict" is necessary for change and growth and that "We undergo our most profound change and grow most deeply when we encounter difference and work on conflict or differences in connection."[2] I would go one step further to suggest that many acts of indirect aggression could be prevented, or at least de-escalated, if we had the skills to constructively communicate directly. When a critical mass of women in the organization has the awareness,

TABLE 7. Sample vision statement and code of conduct

Vision statement

The women of [this organization] are a community of high-performing women who support each other to realize our own potential and the potential of our teams and to provide exceptional service to our clients.

Code of conduct

To realize our vision, we

- Surface our friendship rules—we talk about our expectations

- Stay present and engaged with each other, even in the face of disappointment

- Give each other feedback about the impact of our behaviors

- Are trustworthy—we transknit, but we do not gossip

- Maintain confidences when asked to do so or else say we cannot

- Celebrate and acknowledge each other's achievements

- Compete for rewards and resources while affirming our relationships

- Engage in meaningful disagreement and listen to each other

- Challenge ideas, not people

- Help each other feel heard in meetings

- Self-disclose to the degree we are each comfortable

- Are authentic—we share where we are directly to each other

- Ask ourselves, "What else could be true?" when we feel judgmental of another woman

shared vision, code of conduct, and skills for constructively dealing with differences, we can help each other grow and break out of old patterns.

A key concept here is constructive direct communication. While many women say that dealing directly with conflict is uncomfortable for them, many of my clients say that they have no trouble being direct. However, their style of being direct is one that, relationally, does more harm than good. They think that being direct means to discharge, or dump, their intense feelings all over the other party and make statements full of judgment about the other person. Their coworkers often describe them as aggressive, unreasonable, and difficult to work with or trust.

This type of directness creates defensiveness and distance rather than strengthened connections.

Learning to effectively use feedback skills can clear up misunderstandings and build connections. These skills can be learned as part of the all-woman retreats described previously or in separate skill-building workshops. Effective feedback skills are essential to being able to implement a code of conduct, which is why they are an important part of building a supportive community within an organization, and not just a facet of interpersonal skills.

One of the reasons that good feedback skills can help strengthen relationships is that they help the offended person speak about the personal impact of someone else's behavior in a way that owns and describes the impact but does not blame or judge. The "magic formula" in table 8 provides a guideline for the components of effective feedback, which are to describe specific behaviors, use "I" statements to describe your reaction or thoughts when the behavior happened, and name the feelings that came up for you when the interaction occurred.

Note that the intention of giving the feedback is to improve the relationship, not to vent and discharge for the sake of hurting someone else or to "give someone a piece of my mind." The receiver of the feedback also has a role to play for the feedback to be effective. She has the difficult challenge of really hearing and acknowledging the impact of her behavior without explaining her intention or otherwise defending herself. She doesn't have to agree; she just has to "get it" about the impact she had on the other person and acknowledge that she heard it or ask clarifying questions to be sure she understood it. After the giver of the feedback feels heard and understood, the receiver can tell about her intentions—but not too soon. Pause and breathe, and then explain. Table 8 gives a summary of the important elements of an effective feedback process.

Once a strong community of women has been developed in the organization through awareness building, creation of a shared vision and code of conduct, and skill development for feedback skills, it is time for collective action to identify the policies and practices that could be creating the systemic conditions that encourage indirect and

TABLE 8. Feedback process

"Feedback" definition
Information about past behavior offered in the present that may impact future behavior

Giving feedback	Receiving feedback
• Describe specific behaviors ("When you said or did..."), rather than make general statements ("You always...").	• Paraphrase major parts of what was said to check for clarity and ask, "Did I get it?"
• Describe behaviors the receiver has control over and can choose to change.	• Ask clarifying questions, such as "Are you saying...?"
• Name feelings (mad, sad, glad, scared, loving, etc.).	• Differentiate between intent and impact (see below).
• Own the impact of the receiver's behaviors. Use "I" statements.	• Consider the feedback and take what is useful.
• Do not give advice.	• Listen for patterns, asking youself, "Have I heard any of this feedback before?"
• Check for clarity.	*Note: The intention is to focus on understanding impact while putting aside the reflex to explain intent.*
• Make sure feedback is as timely as possible.	
Note: The intention is to build relationships—not to discharge.	

"Magic formula" for giving effective feedback
When you _____ (describe behavior), the impact on me was _____ (reactions, thought process). I felt _____ (name the feeling—not "I feel that...").

career aggression. The next section will consider some steps to begin this assessment of the organizational culture to build a case for change.

Assessment of the Policies and Practices of the Organization

If your organization has a diversity plan and active support structures working to create an inclusive organizational culture, then your group of women should be able to connect to those structures to focus attention on the policies and practices that impact women specifically, taking all our differences into account, of course. If, however, no such program is in place or it is inactive, the community of women that has been built during the all-woman retreats can become the initial source of information from which to build a case for a broader organizational assessment. If no retreats have been possible, then informal groups can also form to collect stories from their colleagues about the organization's policies and practices to build a business case for change to take to leaders. This group of women can work together to become the driving force for change.

Three common assessment methods can be used to collect data from the community of women, and eventually from the broader employee population, to begin to describe the organization's culture: questionnaires, interviews, and focus groups.[3] Questionnaires can give a big picture of employee attitudes and beliefs, descriptions of and satisfaction with organizational norms and values, and management practices and policies related to systems of accountability, reward, and decision making. Interviews can give more in-depth information about these same areas, and focus groups can generate a conversation among groups of women that both raises their awareness and provides a rich description of the conditions that help or hinder our relationships.

Using any two or all three of these methods can provide the data with which to build a good case for studying and changing policies and practices in the organization. Usually, no one in the organization has the whole picture of how the policies and practices, which tend to evolve in a piecemeal fashion over many years, are interacting to affect groups of people differently. These policies and practices almost always reflect the masculine workplace values described in chapter 1 (see table 2). For example, in the context of a focus group in a client organization, women were able to share their stories about being reprimanded and denied promotions because they managed their projects using feminine workplace values of collaboration and team focus. They were told they needed to demonstrate more leadership decisiveness by not "wasting time" consulting their teams. These stories became the data that helped make a case for engaging the whole organization in a dialogue around the need to examine the assumptions behind the masculine workplace values that got rewarded in order to change these policies and practices.

In an example of a discriminatory policy mess, a focus group in another client organization brought together the stories of individual women, who did not previously know each other. It became clear that policies against part-time work and against working from home had a differential impact on new mothers. (New fathers were afraid to consider even asking to work from home.) The policy said that since part-time employment was not allowed, new mothers could work from home part-time but were expected to work the rest of the time in the office to put in full-time hours—but they could get paid only for the time they were in the office since working from home did not count as official work time. So they worked full-time but only got part-time pay. The policymakers quickly realized, when they saw the results from the focus groups, that this was not a good policy, and was also probably not legal. The implications of this combination of policies had not been visible to them before the women's stories were collected in focus groups. With the use of these data-collection methods, perceptions of unfair policies and practices can be brought to the surface and combined to make the case for change in a way that one voice or one story cannot.

While I am suggesting that a community of women can take the lead in making the case for or starting a process of organizational assessment, it is useful to eventually engage an external consultant to work with the organization for a full assessment. Women within the organization may be professionally vulnerable when delivering bad news to senior leaders, whereas an external person is not. A full-fledged assessment is time consuming, and the community of women is unlikely to have the time or the expertise needed. Yet initiating and continuously monitoring this change process is an invaluable role that needs to be played by these women if real change is to be implemented and sustained.

We have considered some initial steps to begin creating the systemic awareness and the support structures to disrupt the old patterns of indirect and career aggression. We also looked at some ways to start a process of assessing the organizational policies and practices that can trigger horizontal violence between women. Now let's move to the interpersonal level—what to do when you are personally on the receiving end of indirect or career aggression.

Interpersonal Interventions

When you are on the receiving end of indirect aggression, it is important to approach the other person with the intention of staying in and improving your relationship. You have control only over your own actions and intentions, but you can give the other person the benefit of the doubt and take steps to stop the offending behavior and clear up any misunderstandings. It is another matter, however, when you are on the receiving end of career aggression. Here are some things you can do in both situations.

Indirect Aggression—What You Can Do

Remember—we are dealing with very old, deeply buried patterns of behavior, and some of these behaviors will thoughtlessly pop out of us sometimes, even when we have made a commitment to stop. For this reason, we all need to be open to feedback about our actions. Hopefully, every woman you work with is open as well. Sometimes, however, someone may not be at a time in her life, or at a moment in her day, when she is able to be open to feedback about something she has done. We will consider actions to take both when the person is open and when she is not open to working on her relationship with you in the face of your experience of indirect aggression.

Indirect aggression, intentionally hurtful and denied, is subtle and can take many forms. It can take the form of gossip that is judgmental. It can also be a remark or tone of voice that seems sarcastic or nonverbal body language that seems to communicate an intention to exclude or judge or dismiss. When you experience any of these behaviors directed at you, it is important to give feedback to the offending party as soon as possible about the impact of her behavior on you.

Denial is part of indirect aggression, so the aggressor might not admit, either to you or to herself, that she has done anything to you. And it's always possible that you misread or misunderstood the interaction. Nonetheless, for the sake of having a good relationship with you going forward, she may be open to hearing your feedback and taking it in, and you should give her the feedback for the sake of improving the relationship. Even without an admission of guilt or an apology from her, receiving your feedback may help her resolve to refrain from behaving that way in the future, so it is always worth asking for a feedback meeting.

Sometimes the indirect aggression can have such a hurtful impact that stronger measures are needed to repair the relationship. In that case, the relational resilience tool, described in chapter 4, would be more appropriate than simple feedback because it involves an outside party and a more structured process.

The Mother-Sister-Daughter Triangle: A Tool for Identifying Projections between Women

One more situation to consider is when you perceive that indirect aggression has occurred but the offending party is not willing or able to engage with you directly about it. The goal is still to try to maintain a connection with that person. What you can do in this situation is to identify any projections that could be involved, using the Mother-Sister-Daughter triangle.[4]

The core roles of mother, sister, and daughter are universal influences in our development as women, and the triangle is an archetypal structure reflecting the interdependent aspects of these influences (see figure 1).[5] It seems likely that this collective experience of women in one or more of these roles informs many of our relationships with other women. Every woman knows the experience of being a daughter. Although not all women have the experience of being a mother or a sister, most women hold some idealized image of mother and sister in their psyche. These experiences or idealizations are often so potent that we project them onto others. They can influence everyday behavior in individual women. The phenomenon of the mother-sister-daughter triangle becomes a

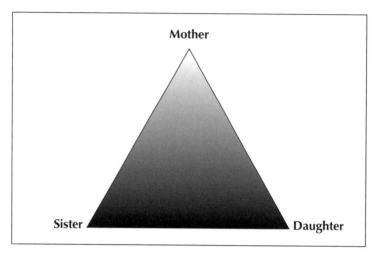

Figure 1. Mother-sister-daughter triangle: A tool for identifying projections between women

lens through which our relationships with other women can be viewed, especially when we are trying to make sense of extreme reactions to another woman—positive or negative, adoration or detestation.

To use the mother-sister-daughter lens effectively, you must have some understanding of where you might be caught in the triangle with the other woman to whom you are having a strong reaction. Does she remind you of your mother or sister or daughter? If you can see a connection between how this woman has behaved toward you and an early experience you had, you might come to feel less offended by her. As an example, I felt that a woman I had known professionally, Cheryl, had treated me unfairly, and she had not responded to my requests to discuss the offending incident at the time. Several years went by, and I was not happy to walk into a new organization and see her working there. I felt that I could not trust her because of what happened in the past, and I told other people not to trust her either. I kept my distance from her. I could not see that I was also behaving in an untrustworthy manner by making demeaning comments about her to others. I could only see that she was someone who had done me wrong.

After some time in the same organization (and avoiding her), I learned about the mother-sister-daughter triangle in a women's leadership training course, and I applied it to my relationship with Cheryl. I asked myself whom Cheryl reminded me of in my family. It took some time for me to realize that she reminded me of one of my sisters, who had tried to physically harm me when we were young. I had put Cheryl in the dangerous sister part of the triangle. As soon as I realized I had done that, an amazing thing happened. It was like a curtain lifted and I could see Cheryl for who she really was. I stopped feeling negative about her. We were never able to reconstruct exactly what had happened all those years ago, but she no longer felt untrustworthy to me. She turned out to be a very nice woman who was not my dangerous sister. This was a projection that I had put on her that was not actually about her at all.

We have considered actions we can take to strengthen relationships in the face of indirect aggression. Career aggression, however, requires a different goal and approach.

Career Aggression: What You Can Do to Stop It

When you feel you are or may be experiencing career aggression, this is not the time to focus on strengthening relationships—remember, you may not know who is trying to damage your career, and if you do know who it is, you may not have a relationship with the person to begin with, as previously described. Your goal, now, needs to be to stop the damaging behavior and to protect your reputation and your career. To achieve these goals, you must be very cautious and thorough in the steps you take as soon as you suspect that someone is trying to damage your career. Keep the circle of people whom you talk to about what is happening very small so that the aggressor does not realize you are preparing to take action. You need to be the one who comes forward first. Here are five suggested steps to take:

Step 1: Write down the story of what is happening to you. Even if you are not completely sure yet what is happening or who is involved, document the following in your own words:

- Whom you talked to

- What you noticed or heard
- When you had each observation or conversation or learned a piece of information

The rule of thumb is to create a detailed record of who, what, and when as soon as you begin to feel that something might be going on that is directed at damaging you. Keep these notes with you and do not leave them lying on your desk or easily accessible in your desk because someone who might spread the information around or who might personally be involved in trying to damage you could see them. You will eventually bring this record with you to HR to provide facts for your case.

Step 2: Do your homework. Research your organization's Equal Employment Opportunity (EEO) statement, employee code of conduct, and harassment policy to understand your rights. Download them from the organization's website, or obtain them from the Human Resources Department. Underline the sections that seem to cover your situation and add them to the folder of materials that you are keeping with you. Every organization has policies and statements that reflect its legal obligation to provide a work environment for all employees that is free from harassment and protects employees from working in a hostile work environment. If someone is trying to damage your career, that person is creating a hostile work environment for you. Your request for help to stop the unwelcome behavior directed at damaging your reputation and career will be taken more seriously when you can show you have done your homework and understand your rights as an employee.

Step 3: Seek out a trusted advisor. It is important that you talk with someone whom you trust to have an unbiased view. This person can help you think through how you will proceed and help you put together your talking points if you are going to confront the aggressor or file an official complaint. You may know a person in HR whom you feel can be your trusted advisor and keep your conversations confidential until you decide what action you are going to take. If not, a trusted advisor can also be any of the following: (1) someone at work who can advise you (2) a family member who is not biased or emotionally involved, or

(3) a professional, such as a clergy member or a therapist with whom you have a good relationship.

Step 4: Confront the career aggressor. If at all possible, confront your aggressor in front of a witness before you officially file a complaint. Plan your talking points with your trusted advisor, and confront your aggressor in a private setting with a witness at your side. The aggressor may admit that she has been acting to damage you, or she may not. In either case, record what happens in the conversation in your detailed notes, as well as any subsequent actions the person might take to try to threaten you to keep you from filing a complaint.

Step 5: Have a confidential conversation with a management- or director-level HR person. Discuss filing a complaint and show the person your detailed record. Discuss steps to escalate your complaint to the next level and ask for her or his advice. It is your decision whether or not to take the next steps. If you decide to go forward with filing a formal complaint, the organization must conduct an investigation. Whether or not the organization is able to prove that the accused person did try to damage your career, this fluid process is very likely to stop the career aggression and restore your reputation.[6]

This process is summarized in table 9.

You can take steps, sometimes alone and sometimes with others, both to shift the relationship dynamics between you and someone else and to help make changes to improve the environment for women on a

TABLE 9. How to stop career aggression

Step 1: Create a detailed record: who, what, and when.

Step 2: Research the organization's EEO statement, employee code of conduct, and harassment policy.

Step 3: Seek out a trusted advisor.

Step 4: Confront the career aggressor.

Step 5: Speak with a director-level HR professional about filing a complaint.

---

system level in your organization. There are also times when, in the case of career aggression, you may just need to protect yourself.

NEXT STEPS

Skills and knowledge are the building blocks for preventing damage to relationships and to your career. The steps below will help prepare you for both.

1. Practice feedback skills as much as you can. As with any skills, they get easier with practice. You can practice giving positive feedback to family members, friends, or coworkers so that you are ready to give negative feedback when the need arises. Be sure to include all the important elements of effective feedback: specific behavior, reaction (thoughts), and feelings. Each component gives a different type of information about the impact of a person's behavior, and they are all important.

2. Practice using the mother-sister-daughter triangle. Notice when you have strong reactions to another woman, either positive or negative, and ask yourself where you have placed her in the triangle. Whom does she remind you of?

3. Investigate the current support structures in your organization for strengthening a women's community, for learning and creating a shared vision and code of conduct, and for assessing the company's policies and procedures. Is there a diversity effort? An existing women's forum? If yes, get involved in the program committee. If not, get a group of women together, including women bosses, for a monthly lunch or dinner and talk about how to shift the patterns to support each other more. Discuss the company policies and practices, and consider how you might develop a business case to present to the leaders about changes that are needed.

4. Research the EEO and harassment policies in your organization. Every organization has them. Be aware of what they say and know your rights.

7

Culture Matters:
Differences Make a Difference

How are we different? Let us count the ways.

Our experiences in organizations are influenced by how gender interacts with race, class, ethnicity, level of employment, sexual orientation, and nationality for every individual woman—just to name a few possible differences.[1] And we cannot assume that our experiences as women in US organizations are the same as those of women in other countries. So far, we have focused on some things that we may have in common as women in organizations, but this book would be incomplete without an honest look at our differences. In this chapter, we will consider some ways to keep both our differences and our commonalities in focus so that we can work together.

Gender Plus[2]

To understand how gender interacts with other differences to impact our experiences as women in organizations, we need a metaphor for seeing these interactions. Evangelina Holvino, a scholar on this topic, suggests that we imagine a hologram or a prism with gender at the center and many sides representing at least race, class, ethnicity, sexual orientation, and nationality.[3] We can see through the prism, and as we turn it, we see all the differences at the same time, but each angle highlights a different combination. In this way, we get a fuller and more holistic view of the experience of gender for women in organizations, and we can better understand each other.[4] We can turn the prism to change what needs to be in focus when we are asking different questions or when the context changes.

Holvino gives us Justice Sonia Sotomayor as an example of how the prism metaphor can help us see wholeness.[5] Sotomayor was nominated for the Supreme Court in 2009 by President Obama. She was confirmed and sits on the court as the third woman, and first Hispanic, Supreme Court justice in the history of the United States. She embraces her race, "Nuyorican" ethnicity,[6] gender, poor working-class background, Ivy League education, and childhood diabetes as simultaneously important contributors to her identity and her view of the world. As we turn the prism, we can see how her perspective on social issues that might come before the court could be uniquely informed and enriched by her combination of life experiences. Every turn of the prism gives her a different understanding of how our country's laws impact the people.

Each Supreme Court justice has a unique prism that shapes her or his perspective, but in the past, too many of the justices had had very similar experiences. To further the case for the value of diverse perspectives, we can look to the United States Senate. In 2012, the Senate had twenty women senators, the most ever in our history. Because there were more women senators, the issue of sexual assault in the military was finally put on the Senate agenda in 2013 for serious debate and action when new information on assaults surfaced. Rather than pushing aside the issue, as it did for decades when multiple scandals occurred—such as the US Navy Tailhook scandal in 1991—Congress passed significant new legislation in 2013 to reform the way sexual assault in the US military is prevented and responded to. When different people are in leadership roles, different issues are put on the agenda, and different decisions are made.

Another example was the ability of a coalition of Democratic and Republican women senators to put forward proposals that broke through the stalemate in the Senate to ultimately end the government shutdown of 2013 and lift the debt ceiling to avoid American default. Although the Senate is still dominated by men, women on both sides of the partisan divide have been able to work together and become a driving force for action in a highly polarized Senate. Senator Susan Collins explained, "Although we (women) span the ideological spectrum, we are used to working together in a collaborative way."[7]

We have been looking at the prism metaphor with gender at the center. Why put gender at the center of the prism? Truly, we could put any dimension of difference—race, class, sexual orientation, or nationality—at the center. The value of putting gender at the center of the prism for this discussion is that gender has been one of the major structures of domination throughout history in every society.[8] Elizabeth Janeway, a scholar who writes about marginalization, identifies women as the oldest and largest marginalized group globally.[9] Another scholar, Lynn O'Brien Hallstein, explains that women have been systematically exploited, oppressed, devalued, and excluded in all capitalist patriarchal systems.[10] So there is value in looking at gender as the core of women's identities because there are threads of a shared experience in organizations around which we can connect. The paradox is that we cannot really connect around a shared identity as women until we can also understand and acknowledge our differences. We can both generalize and leave room to acknowledge differences at the same time by "zooming in and zooming out" from general to specific as we consider our commonalities and the different realities for women in organizations.[11]

Women Come into Organizations Differently as Women

We bring our differences with us into organizations. Scholars have written about the ways that women come into organizations with different definitions of what it means to be a woman.[12] Lyn Mikel Brown, a researcher on gender differences, describes her insights into how white women and women of color defined womanhood and femininity differently: "They spoke differently about fear, conflict, vulnerability, learning, anger."[13]

In fact, focusing on gender can be less important than race, ethnicity, or nationality for many women of color. For lesbians in my study, especially lesbians of color, sexual orientation and race had higher priority for them than gender in terms of both identity and areas of focus or concern. Transgender people face additional hurdles to being included and accepted because they challenge our notion of gender identity as fixed at birth. For many immigrant women, language barriers and the complexities of immigration status for either themselves or their family members can be a primary focus rather than gender.

We enter organizations differently in many other ways—for example, more white women are married than black women, while black women suffer more isolation in their personal lives and have more responsibility for extended families.[14] With less support and more responsibility, black women have more demands on their finite amount of energy. Holvino writes about the ways that many Latinas and Asians carry "cultural scripts" into organizations that conflict with expectations of 24/7 availability and aggressive displays of competence and ambition.[15] Their cultures place a strong value on close family relationships, putting the needs of family before their own careers.

Because of the differences we bring with us, the issues that we think are important as women are not the same. For example, the African American women in my study noted that the concept of "work-life balance," so often raised as an issue by white women in organizations, is a foreign concept to them. Their mothers never had the luxury of staying at home with their children, and neither did their grandmothers or great-grandmothers. Even the concept of "equal pay for equal work," focused on men being paid more than women for the same work, doesn't ring true as the whole picture for women of color. Let's take a look at how the issue of equal pay has a different reality for women of color and lesbians.

Organizations Treat Different Women Differently

Statistics released by the Center for American Progress and the National Women's Law Center tell a story about our different treatment that is usually invisible in both media reports and organizational statistics.[16]

While it is true that, in general, the wages of working women continue to lag behind the pay of their male counterparts, for women of color the pay gap is double and possibly triple the size. To start with, as a group, women of color earn less than their white female peers.

American women who work full-time, year round, are paid only 77 cents for every dollar paid to their male counterparts, but this is not the whole story. Among women of color working full-time, year round, African American women are paid only 64 cents and Hispanic women only 55 cents for every dollar paid to white non-Hispanic men. When we look more closely at the differences between women's pay, we see that the typical African American woman working full-time, year round, is paid roughly 83 cents for every dollar paid to her white non-Hispanic female counterpart. Hispanic women working full-time, year round, are paid just 72 cents for every dollar paid to their white non-Hispanic female counterpart.

Unfortunately, even this is not all the bad news for women of color. They are also paid less than the men in their own racial or ethnic groups. The typical African American woman working full-time, year round, is paid roughly 85 cents for every dollar paid to her African American male counterpart. Hispanic women are paid 91 cents for every dollar paid to their Hispanic male counterparts. In fact, women of all major racial and ethnic groups earn less than men of the same group. The largest gap is within the Asian American communities, where women earn 73 cents for every dollar earned by Asian American men.

Many people think that these income discrepancies are a vestige of some ancient history that is fading out, but statistics tell us that these inequities are still being perpetuated for younger workers. The American Association of University Women reports that millennial women—those born between 1978 and 2000—are paid 82 cents for every dollar paid to their male peers. Even when controlling for factors such as the type of degree earned, the type of occupation right out of college, and hours worked on the job, researchers found a significant pay discrepancy across the board between millennial women and millennial men.[17]

Lesbians of color struggle even more with issues of pay inequity, reflecting the cumulative impact of multiple categories of disadvantage—in this case, gender, sexuality, and race. Working gay and transgender people of color earn less than their heterosexual and white gay and transgender counterparts. Black same-sex couples also significantly lag behind white same-sex couples in median income.

Women Carry Other Differences into Organizations

Are you clueless about the ways differences shape the perspectives of your coworkers? Author Tom Finn reminds us that while many differences are visible, many are not, and our ability to connect with and support each other may depend on understanding the histories we carry into the workplace, often generationally.[18] For example, I am white and a secular Jew. While I do not practice the religion, being Jewish is an important identity in my prism. I carry with me a history of my own painful experiences of anti-Semitism from my childhood in Kansas. I also carry with me the images of the holocaust in Europe that my parents made sure I saw while I was growing up so that I would never forget what happened to Jews. This combination of events that happened before I was born and during my own childhood means that, even now, I always scan my environment to see who else might be Jewish so that I know whom I can feel safe with. Because I do not "look Jewish" or have a recognizably Jewish name, I can take a long time to reveal this side of my identity to new people until I get a sense of their attitudes and degree of cluelessness. I have gotten feedback from coworkers that I can seem standoffish when people first meet me. They cannot see this invisible difference that is part of what makes me tick.

Many of us carry in some current and some historical differences that can make it difficult to connect with us. Some of us are from alcoholic families or abusive families or are rape survivors, and we may find it difficult to trust people—but these are invisible differences. I find that white women are often clueless about the long history of betrayal by white women of black women during slavery times in this country, about which many black women are still resentful. Many black women feel unsupported by white women who do not join them to fight against racial profiling outside and racial discrimination inside organizations (among many other race-based injustices). They find it difficult to join white women to focus on gender-based inequities when white women do not make working against racial injustice an equal priority.

Another example of how we can carry history in comes from the experiences of Chicanas and Latinas. We may not know that a second- or third-generation US-born Chicana or Latina carries with her the stories from her parents and grandparents of abusive and oppressive treatment by whites that leave her ambivalent, at best, about expecting or offering support to white women colleagues. And we may be clueless about the shame still carried by a Japanese American colleague about the internment of her family by the US government during World War II. She may seem distant or difficult to connect with if we do not know how history has shaped her prism.

Not only do we carry in differences that affect our ability to connect across groups, but differences within groups can affect us as well. For example, a secular Jew like me can feel judged and rejected by religious Jews. Women can also feel distanced from each other within groups because of class-of-origin differences. For example, two African American women attended a workshop I recently facilitated. One of the women took a big risk in the group and made a statement about race that she knew would be controversial. It was, indeed, controversial, and she took a lot of flak from the predominantly white group—alone. During the break I asked the other African American woman why she didn't offer any support to her colleague, and she said something like, "She's always had it easy and thinks she's 'all that,' so I just didn't feel like helping her out." With a little more conversation, it became clear that even though they were currently peers professionally, their different class backgrounds—one working class and one upper-middle class—created a reflex to let a coworker stand alone, unsupported. I submit that class differences create this reflex within many, if not all, groups. Class differences, colorism (where lighter skin and "good hair" are more valued), and other differences within groups can create distance, even though group members outwardly appear to share a common dimension of diversity.[19]

So far in this chapter, we have looked at how some differences can affect us in the workplace in a US context. Now we will take a look at how some of these issues may have a different meaning in other countries.

Transnational Differences

We should never assume that we know how women in other places in the world see race, class, gender, sexual orientation, and other differences. Many of us work in multinational organizations, and though corporate cultures create some shared ways of thinking, we still cannot assume that the women with whom we interact in other countries share our views of what is important. For one thing, histories of colonialism and imperialism have left behind sensitivities and psychic scars that may have shaped their prisms in ways that are unfamiliar to those of us who are white Westerners. Women located in other countries may actually see us as representatives of the colonizers and find it difficult to trust us. You will see why if you consider that by 1914, Europe held a grand total of roughly 85 percent of the earth as colonies, protectorates, dependencies, dominions, and commonwealths. Only Japan escaped colonization.[20]

The legacy of colonialism and imperialism comes from the psychic and physical damage inflicted when both slavery and published colonial "contracts" claimed the right of Europeans and the United States to rule over the peoples of Mexico, Central America, South America, Asia, Africa, and the Pacific and to enslave Native Americans and Africans based on "moral superiority." The conquering Europeans and, later, the United States, saw the societies they took over as "deficient" and the natives as "childlike and incapable of self rule."[21] The result was what Amina Mama describes as a "pigmentocracy," in which "elaborate distinctions were made between people on the basis of their racial ancestry and physical attributes. This placed pure white at the apex of a complex listing of the races and pure African at the bottom."[22] The lingering impact of these experiences, generations later, should not be underestimated.

At the same time, local differences in customs, political structures, and laws can also produce different meanings. For example, the women in my research who live in China explained that the one-child policy in China is a big factor in organizations. Members of the younger generation of workers are looking for friends at work because they have no siblings. They blend family and work "without constraint" because they need emotional bonds. In comparison, members of the older generation have siblings so they get their emotional needs met by their family outside of work. The older workers keep a clear separation between family and work. Because of the one-child policy, it is more difficult for an older manager to motivate younger workers because they do not need to earn as much money since they have fewer family obligations. At the same time, younger women feel intense pressure to have a child because they fear being criticized if they do not—having a child is very precious in the one-child environment.

We need to ask many questions to fully understand the ways that gender may have varied meanings in interaction with race, ethnicity, class, sexuality, age, ability, religion, and other differences both within and across national contexts. For example, are ethnicity and caste more meaningful for women in India than race? What significance does education have in social relations between women? What ethnic or tribal differences have significance, and how do they affect women's relationships within a country or across a region? What is the importance of individual achievement versus family and community approval? How do the predominant religious beliefs, in a national context, impact opportunities for women? What laws and practices about sexual identity impact opportunity? How do patterns of accumulated disadvantage, reflected in occupation and income statistics in a national context, inform us of different meanings? These are just a few of the questions we can ask to become aware of how gender may mean something different in other contexts.

Working Together across Differences

We can acknowledge both our differences and our commonalities as women. In fact, many of us must feel that our differences are seen and acknowledged by others before we are open to discovering any common goals as women.[23] This is especially true for those of us who are not members of the dominant group of women—that is, those who are not straight white women. How does my gender interact with my race, sexual identity, and other factors to create my experience in the organization in ways that are different from your experience? We need to understand this for ourselves so that we can help others see us and also hear how this works for other women—both others within our own racial or ethnic group and across groups. Once we can see our differences, we can understand how to support each other in meaningful ways and work together toward common goals.

Two ways to move toward understanding our differences as women are to meet in all-woman retreats for awareness-raising workshops and to engage in joint projects between affinity groups in the organization.

Awareness-Raising Workshops in All-Female Retreat Settings

After the initial all-woman retreats to gain an awareness of systemic gender dynamics and develop a shared vision and code of conduct (see chapter 6), a next level of all-woman retreats, possibly in smaller, mixed groups, can be held to explore and share differences and identify some common goals for working together to change the organization. These conversations work best, at least initially, when guided by a professional facilitator who is experienced at communicating across differences. The facilitator may structure exchanges between various groups that include topics such as

- What we feel is important for other women to know about our group

- What we value and don't want to lose about our group

- One difficult question we have for one of the other groups

- Something we think we all care about changing in our organization.

These structured conversations can result in the discovery of common ground and an understanding of differences that paves the way for joining forces to work together for change.

Joint Projects between Affinity Groups

Sometimes affinity groups formally exist in organizations, such as one for women managers, one for African Americans, one for Asian Americans, one for Latinos, one for LGBT (lesbian, gay, bisexual, and transgender) employees, and others. However, these groups may not see the other groups as having the same interests or goals. It can be helpful if affinity groups can define joint projects, even if their scopes are small, to open the possibility of building trust and taking on larger projects later.

In one of my client groups, a group of senior-level women decided to try to get the women in the organization together by organizing a women's leadership forum as a one-day annual event where fun and leadership development opportunities would be shared and trust could be built. Not unusually, most of the women of color in this organization worked in support roles, and many women in technical positions worked in the field as the only woman on their teams. Not surprisingly, the first year of the forum, only a small number of women, predominantly white professionals, accepted the invitation to the event. The support women didn't feel the event was for them, even though everyone was invited. Some technical women reported that they would not attend because they felt they would be disloyal to their male colleagues if they attended. Others felt their male managers would penalize them if they attended and decided not to go. But the original organizers kept their focus on getting the women of the company more connected, and each year the attendance grew.

The women of color went from one table of women sitting in the corner and not participating in the experiential activities at the first annual event to a much larger group of women mixing and mingling with others by the fourth year. By the fourth year, about two-thirds of the women in the company attended the forum. It may seem that a one-day event held once a year would be too insignificant to have an impact, but the environment did begin to change as a mentoring program was spontaneously and informally launched by some of the more senior women for junior women and some of the isolated technical women in the field began to meet periodically and offer each other support.

Within four years, more women of color began showing up in the ranks of the technical and professional women. To be sure, pressure on the organizational culture to change came from sources other than this one-day event. Small groups of more senior technical and professional women were involved in an intensive one-year women's leadership training program during this same period, which greatly enhanced their ability to support other women.

In this chapter, we looked at gender plus the other differences we bring into organizations and considered ways that gender interacts with other differences to impact our perceptions and our experiences in organizations. We have so many differences, yet there are ways to acknowledge them and also identify common interests as women in organizations. Discovering ways to support each other across differences is difficult and requires that we be intentional about understanding how we each see the world differently. Differences do make a difference, but we can all go further in our lives and careers if we can find the pathway to supporting each other in the face of those differences.

NEXT STEPS

When we can understand ourselves and connect across differences with other women, we release energy for creativity and innovation in the workplace. The practices below will help you gain comfort and skill for developing these relationships.

1. Identify the sides on your prism that are most relevant for you at this time in your life and career, keeping gender in the center. For example, I might ask myself how being a Jewish woman, white woman, US-born woman, and woman in my sixties are all currently impacting my experience. What is important for others to know about me as I turn the prism that reflects my wholeness?

2. Make a list of the sides of your prism. Reflect on how each side interacts with being a woman for you at this time in your life and career.

3. Become more curious and open to learning about the experiences of other women who are different. Listen to understand, and be willing to share your experience.

4. Make a connection once a month with someone from a different culture whom you don't usually interact with. Cultural differences can include different employment levels, ages, races, nationalities, religions, and other differences.

5. Read the histories of other groups or watch movies about the experiences of women from different cultures, such as *Real Women Have Curves.*

8

Case Examples and Conclusions

What? So What? Now What?

We have considered many ways that the interaction of subtle patterns, unspoken assumptions, and organizational structures and practices can create misunderstandings and confusion between women in the workplace, as well as barriers for our success. We also considered some strengths in our relational practices that we can feel quite good about. These positive patterns are not currently valued in organizations but need to be claimed and celebrated by us and recognized as value-added practices by organizations.

In chapter 1, we considered the ways that women unconsciously carry unspoken egalitarian friendship rules, or relational expectations, into the workplace where they clash with masculine hierarchical norms and values. We considered the potential for disappointment in and damage to our workplace relationships when our expectations of each other are unconscious and unnamed.

Double binds for women bosses was the focus of chapter 2, including the impossible position that women bosses are in when they cannot be considered both competent and likeable. We also discussed the systemic pressures on women to not support other women, especially at the more senior levels in organizations.

The boundary confusion that is the natural outcome of women's workplace values and women's friendship rules was the topic of chapter 3. In this chapter, we discussed both the benefits and the drawbacks of fluid boundaries for women in the workplace—as bosses and as staff. We described a boundary negotiation tool called "role hats," which can play to our relational strengths and enhance our ability to manage role boundaries while staying in a relationship.

In chapter 4, we explored some communication patterns that both serve and do not serve women well in our relationships at work. We considered ways to strengthen the positive communication patterns and eliminate the destructive ones and offered a tool for repairing relationships when damage has happened.

Indirect and career aggression between women, the behaviors related to backstabbing and sabotage, are patterns that are too common—but that happen for a reason. In chapters 5 and 6, we dug into understanding why these patterns happen and how to change or stop them.

In chapter 7, we considered the challenge of holding the awareness of our differences and our commonalities as women and the importance of being able to consider both simultaneously. We took a deep dive into ways that women are different and the importance of being able to acknowledge our differences before we can discover and work together on our mutual interests. In each chapter, we considered steps we can take, individually and interpersonally, to increase trust and strengthen our relationships with women coworkers (see the summary in table 10).

What difference can it make to a group if its members apply the concepts and practices described in this book? Following are six case studies, some of them composites of more than one similar group, that demonstrate how the concepts were applied and the impact that resulted for a work group, two nonprofit boards of directors, two professional development groups, and a professional association. What these groups have in common is that the members were all women and the consultant was the author.

TABLE 10. Tips for increasing trust and collaboration with women at work

- Name and negotiate your friendship expectations and role hats.
- Rename and reclaim your positive patterns.
- Discover your mutuality.
- Name your experience and your feelings.
- Be curious about the other woman's experience and feelings.
- Distinguish gossip from transknitting.
- Notice your projections.

Applications—Some Case Examples

Each of the groups described in the six case studies developed a code of conduct. It is important to distinguish between these codes of conduct and the team norms or team guidelines that are generally recommended for effective teamwork.[1] The codes of conduct suggested in this book were developed within a context of understanding the research on women's relationship dynamics in the patriarchal workplace. The women in these case studies learned about women's friendship rules—including the taboo against discussing our expectations of one another—organizational structures and practices that reward masculine workplace values, patterns of indirect communication for women and conflict avoidance, gossip and transknitting, double binds, and horizontal violence. Only after learning about these structures and patterns and their implications for women's relationships in the workplace did they develop their codes of conduct. They understood that the tensions they experienced and the misunderstandings that occurred were the result of larger system dynamics and that they could change these patterns if they worked together.

An All-Woman Claims-Processing Group

The manager of eight culturally diverse women had come to the end of her rope about how to help her claims-processing group work together. Tensions had developed between two of the women in the unit, and the other members of the unit had, for the most part, taken sides. The situation had gotten so bad that the women had stopped sharing information, so their productivity was affected. The culture of this group had always been one in which there were cliques and gossip—and where conflict was avoided and bad feelings went underground and were expressed behind others' backs. Trust and morale were, not surprisingly, very low.

I shared the concepts about women's patterns of relationship in the workplace and told the women that what they were experiencing was common and was not just about them as a group—and that things could change for the better, if they wanted them to change. The purpose of setting this positive tone was to help them unhook from negative stereotypes about women not being able to trust each other and get along and to give them hope.

We met in two half-day sessions, and at the end of the first session, the women were instructed to do homework overnight and identify some friendship rules that they thought women had, including themselves. They were encouraged to talk with sisters and women friends to discover the friendship rules operating in some of their relationships outside of work. The purpose of this overnight reflection was that, for the most part, our friendship rules are unconscious, and it takes some reflection time to become aware of them.

The next day, I asked the group members to have a discussion of the friendship rules or expectations they were aware of between women in general. The conversation went on for two hours and everyone participated. Each friendship rule that got named was discussed until a shared meaning was established. I facilitated the conversation and asked questions for clarification, and I wrote down each friendship rule as the group came to an agreement about what it meant. Spontaneously, the conversation shifted from friendship rules that women have, in a general sense, to a code of conduct that the group was developing for itself. When the women stepped back and looked at what they had discussed, they liked what they had created and decided what to keep and what not to keep for their own agreements on how they wanted to operate with each other going forward. While I did not label their work as a code of conduct, I suggested that they could decide to live by these agreements for a while as a pilot and then revisit them. They agreed to try this. Their code of conduct included the following elements:

- Communicate with each other openly and express thoughts, feelings, and needs. Don't assume that others know.
- Be direct. Give feedback and be open to receiving it.
- Trust that someone's intentions are good—cut each other some slack.
- Help each other out—all hands on deck.
- Respect boundaries—it's all right to ask for help, but don't assume someone else has the time—ask about her workload.
- Keep each other informed.

Group members later reported a significant shift in the cohesiveness and maturity of the group. They reported engaging in constructive conflict in ways that had never happened before. Trust, morale, and communication all improved significantly.

Two All-Woman Nonprofit Boards of Trustees

Two all-woman boards of trustees were in need of revitalization and refocusing about how to work together. On one board, tensions were high, with factions and gossip causing frustration and low trust for the executive director. In addition, the low energy of board members meant that there was poor follow-through on commitments.

The second board experienced some tensions between members, as well as a deep fear of conflict that meant they were unable to address the tensions and misunderstandings that existed or to make hard decisions. Key members were threatening to resign if the board did not become more authentic and productive, which only served to further paralyze the group.

In both cases, I gave the groups an overview of the research on women's dynamics in the workplace and assured them that what they were experiencing was not unusual and could change. Placing their experience in this larger context allowed the groups to relax a bit and feel hopeful. The concepts of friendship rules, indirect versus direct communication, conflict avoidance, and transknitting grounded them in what was happening and helped them begin to see a pathway to do things differently. By the time we got to the creation of a code of conduct about how they wanted to go forward, they were energized and ready to try something new. Their codes included the following elements:

- Assume good and shared will.
- Be willing to speak our feelings, check out assumptions, and suspend judgment.
- Be listened to without being interrupted, having our sentences finished, or having someone try to convince or direct us.
- Assume there are differences of opinion and invite them, while taking the risk to express our own.
- Give each other appreciation.
- When we take things personally, name it, speak it, and own it.
- Share our perspective and identify it as a "lens" that we have.

Both boards reported significant shifts for the better after their sessions. The executive director of the first board noticed a surge of energy and commitment from her board members. People did what they said they would do, showed up and participated fully in board meetings, and interacted more honestly with each other and with her. The second board reported that members had difficult conversations with each other when they needed to and reminded each other of the importance of speaking the unspoken. Trust increased as honesty increased and energy for the work flowed again in a way that had not been true for quite some time.

Two All-Woman Professional Development Groups

Two all-woman professional development groups developed codes of conduct at the beginning of their life together as groups. The first was a group of twenty-four women participating in a one-year women's leadership development program that met several times during the year. The second group comprised approximately twenty senior and junior women in a new, year-long, mentoring program inside an organization where the senior women were the mentors. A goal in both programs was to strengthen women's ability to support other women as one aspect of leadership.

After presenting the research on women's relationship patterns in the workplace, I worked with each group to develop a code of conduct in the context of the research. The codes included the following elements:

- State our expectations.
- Give others feedback about their impact.
- Stay engaged with each other.
- Be willing to engage in meaningful disagreement.
- Self-disclose to the degree that each of us is comfortable.
- Transknit. Don't gossip.

After the sessions, both groups reported a shift from feeling like loose collections of individuals to feeling like supportive communities. In addition to holding each other to their agreements, the mentoring group agreed to encourage their other women colleagues to behave in these ways as well.

An All-Woman Professional Association

Last, but not least, is a group of women who had been meeting for twenty years—an association of women who work professionally with women as therapists, teachers, body workers, trainers, and consultants. This group was particularly interesting to me because the members had managed to maintain relationships with each other for a very long time, through many challenges. One of their purposes was to continue to learn about women's dynamics by being in this community of women and to continue their professional development together. They invited me to share my research with them as a professional development activity and to help them apply it as a lens for understanding their experience in community.

They had figured out a lot about women's dynamics in the years they were together and had lost some original members along the way as "stuff happened." They learned from these experiences with each other and developed written procedures about how to handle conflicts, money, and other sources of tension. They resonated with the concept of friendship rules and codes of conduct and realized that while they surely had them, both individually and as a group, they had never articulated them to each other. I worked with them to do so.

Because of the longevity of the group, it seemed important to give the women an opportunity to step back and identify the key events in the life of the group over the twenty years that had influenced the formation of the group's current friendship rules or behavioral expectations. We put a blank time line on the wall, and each woman placed sticky notes about key moments or events. We then worked our way along the time line, and the women took turns telling the stories of the key moments and reflecting together on the impact those moments had had on whom they had become as a group.

The group members then reflected individually on what they thought the current friendship rules were for the group—what behaviors they had come to expect from each other. Then pairs and trios formed to merge their lists and find agreement. The pairs and trios then joined with another group and merged their lists, and three merged lists were eventually posted on the walls on large easel paper.

I then gave a brief presentation to the whole group on relational resilience and asked the members to identify the friendship rules on their merged lists that they thought were most responsible for helping them stay in community for so many years. Here are some of the items they identified:

- It's all right to challenge each other.
- We check out our assumptions about each other.
- We witness each other and say, "I see you."
- We sit behind a woman in a difficult conversation so that she feels someone has her back.

- We hang in, especially during struggles and hard times.
- We will mess up with each other. We forgive mess-ups. We expect them and own them.

Once the group had completed this work, the women reflected together on what they had accomplished over the years and felt proud. They also noticed several inconsistencies in their lists and identified these as land mines where future misunderstandings were waiting to happen and further discussion was needed. They were also able to see more clearly where the needs of individuals were in conflict with the culture of the group. One pair of women also reported the next morning that they realized they had some unfinished business with each other and had successfully returned to a conversation they needed to have. Overall, the group members reported that they felt the work had energized the group and brought them together. At the end of the session, they were able to make a decision about bringing in new members that they had been unable to make previously.

A theme for most of the groups in the case studies was that understanding the larger context and patterns that affected their dynamics and creating shared agreements about how to change these patterns was *energizing* for the groups. Energy that the women had previously put into defending or protecting themselves from each other was now available for productive work. Who wouldn't prefer to work in a supportive, trusting environment?

Conclusions

This book has described subtle patterns that my clients and research participants were not conscious of, unspoken assumptions that they did not even know they had, and organizational structures and practices that were invisible to them. The women who participated in the research were not aware that friendship rules act as filters. They could not see the systemic way that masculine workplace cultures set women up to be confused and disappointed by each other. They could not see the impact of internalized negative stereotypes on their relationships. It is important to be able to see these larger forces at play to be able to resist being affected by those forces and strengthen our ability to support each other.

Women need skills for naming and negotiating friendship rules and role boundaries when they are in charge, as well as in peer relationships and when reporting to female bosses. They need skills that will enable them to be explicit about whether they are wearing the hat of a friend, teammate, or boss during interactions where expectations from each other may need to vary. Many women who work in predominantly male teams complain that it is difficult for them to feel heard by their male colleagues. It can feel, then, like a violation of friendship rules if another woman on the team disagrees with them in front of the men in a team meeting—yet it is important for women to be able to express differences of opinion when they are part of a work team. These women could explicitly agree that in mixed-gender team meetings, they are free to disagree with each other. At the same time, they could agree to expect each other to help get their ideas heard by saying something like, "I think we moved away too quickly from consideration of Jane's idea and we should come back to it before we make a decision."

In other situations, women can clarify when they are stepping out of a colleague role and into a friend role where they need empathy, instead of challenge, on a professional level by naming the role switch they are making. Women can develop skills to discuss and agree about what they expect from each other in different roles, make their friendship rules explicit, and negotiate them so that their relationships can survive the need to compete and differentiate as they advance in their careers.

Renaming and reclaiming the positive patterns that build relationships and teams can help us resist internalizing the negative stereotypes (such as "all women are catty and untrustworthy") that set us up against each other. Learning to differentiate between our positive and negative patterns of talk—to embrace our positive patterns, such as transknitting, and stop gossiping—can also help create more trusting and collaborative work environments that will benefit everyone.

Indirect and career aggression between women is the result of both negative societal stereotypes about women and systemic disregard for feminine workplace values that set us up to turn on each other. Paolo Freire called this dynamic "horizontal violence." This behavior, women sabotaging other women, does not reflect something that is "essential" about women. All oppressed groups, or groups that experience systematic exploitation, exclusion, marginalization, and devaluing, act out against members of their own group because they internalize the negative stereotypes about their group and feel powerless to change their situation. Women can transform this behavior by becoming aware that career aggression is a response to our environments and by developing a code of conduct and a positive shared vision about how we want to be in relationship with each other. We can learn to both compete with each other and support each other while maintaining our relationship.

Powerful forces influence our internalizing negative beliefs about women. Yet acting out these beliefs against other women is hurtful. Indirect and career aggression are not unconscious acts. However, if we are not able to see the systemic forces operating on us and do not have the skills to name and negotiate our friendship rules and role boundaries to change what we are doing, these patterns, deeply rooted in childhood and adolescence, will continue. Choices come from awareness of where our patterns come from—we can then decide what we want to keep and what we want to change about our relationships and our organizations.

Both male and female managers need to learn how women's friendship cultures can add value to an organization to enhance morale and productivity among their work groups. By developing skills and a positive shared vision and code of conduct, we can shift the negative dynamics between women and prevent them from occurring. With support from interventions such as retreats, workshops, guest speakers, and coaching, we can empower women, on both the individual and group levels, to disturb the old, destructive patterns that result from our marginalization, join forces to change organizational cultures, and reclaim and cultivate the positive relational dynamics with other women in the workplace (see table 11).

TABLE 11. Summary of organizational change strategies

- Conduct all-woman retreats and workshops to
  - Raise awareness of women's dynamics.
  - Raise awareness of cultural differences.
  - Develop skills.
- Encourage joint projects between affinity groups.
- Form lunch or study groups and include women bosses.
- Provide executive coaching to women and men who supervise women.
- Assess the culture, policies, and practices of the organization for differential impact on women.
- Gather the stories of women in the organization about the differential impact on women of the policies and practices, either formally or informally, to make the "business case" to leaders for the need for change.

APPENDIX

Research Approach and Methods

The research findings presented in this book are from a feminist ethnographic study conducted by the author. An ethnographic study is concerned with describing social and cultural phenomena from an insider's perspective.[1] Triangulation, or the integration of data from multiple sources, is central for ethnographic validity and requires that the ethnographer "compares information sources to test the quality of the information…to understand more completely the part an actor plays…and ultimately to put the whole situation into perspective."[2] The form of analysis used in ethnographic research is sifting and sorting to look for patterns of thought and action and to build theory.

Shulamit Reinharz notes that there is no agreed-upon definition of "feminism" and no research methods that are uniquely feminist.[3] Research methods, such as ethnography, become feminist in the hands of feminists who attend reflexively to the significance of gender. What made this a *feminist* ethnographic study rather than simply an ethnographic study is that not only was I actively involved as a feminist researcher in the production of knowledge, but I also made sure to "continuously and reflexively attend to the significance of gender…understanding the social realities of women as actors."[4] I also used "women's language and behavior to understand the relation between self and context."[5]

What also fundamentally positions this research as a feminist study is the way the relationship between the researcher and the participants is defined. Establishing the participants as collaborators with the researcher rather than as objects of study who do not participate in meaning-making is a specifically feminist approach. During the group meetings, I asked the participants to engage in discussion to interpret their role-plays by asking probing questions such as, "What patterns did you see in these role-plays?" I had a second meeting with some participants from each group to review my initial coding and add further interpretation. To achieve saturation, or fuller coverage of groups or industries, some additional women were interviewed who did not participate in any group session. A feminist ethnographic approach is best suited to the goals of this study, which are to describe the patterns that exist in women's relationship dynamics in the workplace and the meaning that women make of them.

Underlying Research Paradigm

I selected performativity (Erving Goffman's use of theatrical metaphor to elevate socially expected behavior) and collective memory (the way that a dominant culture collectively shapes identity and experience, theories, and methodologies) as platforms for this feminist ethnographic study because of the nature of the phenomena to be studied.[6] Pat O'Connor notes that understanding friendship dynamics between women is at "the heart of our understanding of key issues in women's lives."[7] I submit that friendship dynamics are at the heart of understanding the patterns in women's relationships in the workplace. Yet friendship is a social process that is not conducive to study by survey methodology or focus groups.[8]

Focus groups produce only limited data from women about friendship expectation patterns. This may occur because, as Frigga Haug explains, "Women's experiences are colonized in a particular way by dominant patterns of thought, and by interpretations that organize our subordination."[9] Huang also notes that it is difficult to rationally acknowledge material that is emotional and rooted in the past.[10] Many women have painful experiences with other girls and women in their pasts, and rational processes such as surveys and focus groups are not useful for making these experiences available for study. Haug notes that we must make conscious the ways in which we have "unconsciously interpreted the world" in order to develop resistances, or different patterns of behavior that serve us better as women in patriarchal systems.[11] But bringing our colonized patterns of thought into consciousness can happen only through nonrational processes. For this reason, I used videorecorded group role-plays followed by group interpretive discussions and in-depth interviews as the methodologies for studying patterns of interaction between women in the workplace. These methods are grounded in performativity and collective memory theories.

Performativity Theory

Erving Goffman is credited with first using the metaphor of a theatrical performance as a framework for understanding social interactions. His theory of performativity helps provide the rationale for using group role-plays and interpretive discussions as the methodologies for this study. He explains that the performance of routines, such as interactions between female coworkers, is "'socialized,' molded and modified to fit into the understanding and expectations of the society in which it is presented."[12] In other words, our interactions are performances of how society expects us to behave. The group role-plays in this study are performances that reveal the societal expectations and norms that produce familiar patterns of behavior between women and open the possibility of change.

The goal of this study is not only to contribute to knowledge by describing patterns of interaction between women but also to improve the quality of women's lives, or "to create positive social change."[13] Goffman notes that performance—in this case, role-plays—allows "the reliving of experience."[14] It seems possible then, that the role-plays create an awareness that will result in a positive change in the patterns between women.

Goffman's work provides the rationale for conducting data-collection sessions where there were enough study participants to perform at least two group role-plays. Goffman notes, "When the individual presents himself before others, his performance will tend to incorporate and exemplify the officially accredited values of the society, more so, in fact, than does his behavior as a whole."[15] He explains that at least two teams must present themselves to each other for the values of society to surface, which is why at least two role-play groups were created at each group-research site. Goffman notes that a team performance "creates an emergent team impression which can be treated as fact in its own right, as a third level of fact located between the individual performance on one hand and the total interaction of participants on the other."[16] This third level of fact, or the material of the performances, became the data for the interpretive group discussions.

A rationale for holding in-depth interviews about the interpretive group discussion in the research design comes partially from the work of Dorinne K. Kondo. She not only advocates that performance "is accorded status as ethnographic practice" but also acknowledges that performance "can never be captured fully by text, the camera, or the word; for example, even a videotape of a performance frames it in ways particular to the framing apparatus itself and to the circumstance of filming."[17] In other words, there may be nuances and layers of meaning that are not captured or apparent in the initial session that would become apparent in a follow-up discussion or review of tape segments during interviews by study participants. Additional interviews with women who did not participate in a group session, such as those conducted with additional nurses in this study, can also provide insight into the performance of socially expected routines and the existence of intact-group dynamics. I will provide further rationale for the design in the following section with a review of collective memory theory.

Collective Memory Theory

A number of scholars have written about the role of collective memory in identity creation and maintenance and the role of society and the dominant culture in shaping identity.[18] Haug explains that "experience may be seen as lived practice in the memory of a self-constructed identity...[that] is structured by expectations, norms, and values, in short by the dominant culture."[19] Maurice Halbwachs and Haug agree that "human beings produce their lives collectively," under the pressure of society.[20] Halbwachs adds that the individuals draw on the context of specific groups to remember and, as members of many group identities, have many group contexts to draw from. The group context shared by the participants of this study is that of women, specifically women in the workplace, although other group memberships such as race, nationality, and class could be relevant as well.

Halbwachs explains that the group context helps with remembering: "Our confidence in the accuracy of our impression increases, of course, if it can be supported by others' remembrances also."[21] He provides rationale for conducting this study in a group setting along with conducting individual interviews. In addition, Haug and Halbwachs agree that memory is often unconscious and can be recreated through "third-party mechanisms," or "imaginative reenactments."[22] Haug talks about the importance of getting some distance from past events that were emotionally painful. Role-plays can accomplish this goal of allowing difficult experiences or memories to be recalled and enacted.

Haug provides the rationale for this research design where interpretive group discussion follows role-plays when she notes, "Nor is analysis conceivable in the absence of a collective...spontaneous discussion of any story begun with an implicit comparison, in which one experience was pitted against another."[23] In this research design, the role-plays (a minimum of two) provided the comparison of stories to spark the discussion.

Haug also provides some rationale for conducting follow-up interviews. Her research, based on the collective memory project of a feminist collective in Germany, found that memory is sometimes selective and incomplete, and participants could become defensive about remembering painful events. Only by reflection and writing over a two-year period could patterns in women's socialization be seen by the group members. While this study is much narrower in scope, some period of reflection after the first round of role-plays and discussions seemed to bring richer and deeper insight during follow-up interviews.

The Research Design

Six different groups of women participated in this study. The groups represented a variety of settings: a predominantly male corporate technology environment, a predominantly female healthcare environment, a mixed female and male state and municipal government environment, and three cross-industry groups. In addition to participating in group sessions, some women were also interviewed from each group and some additional women who did not participate in a group session were interviewed to achieve saturation, or more complete coverage. Both group sessions and in-depth interviews were conducted in the United States and in Spain, and additional interviews were conducted with nurses and lesbians in the United States and with mixed-industry professional women in China, Mexico, and India. The participants were all women, and all volunteered to participate in the study. The study was conducted using videorecorded group role-plays, followed by videorecorded group discussions. Interviews were audiorecorded, and half of the in-depth follow-up interviews utilized stimulated recall with video clips from the group session to allow the participants to step back, deepen their reflection, and co-construct the meaning of the enactments.[24] Institutional Review Board (IRB) approval was received, the initial doctoral study was concluded during 2008, and additional data was collected and analyzed through 2012. Figure 2 shows the research design elements and flow.

Between 5 and 40 women participated in each group session, with between two and five role-plays performed by each group. Each woman in a group session participated in only one role-play. A total of 119 women participated in the research. Participants completed a background questionnaire at the end of each group session or interview to allow for sociodemographic self-description of the participants. The research design included analysis of data as it was collected: identification and coding of patterns from the videorecordings, observation and coding of content from the discussions and interviews, and description and tracking of context from field notes.[25]

Potential study participants contacted the researcher directly to indicate that they voluntarily agreed to participate. They signed a

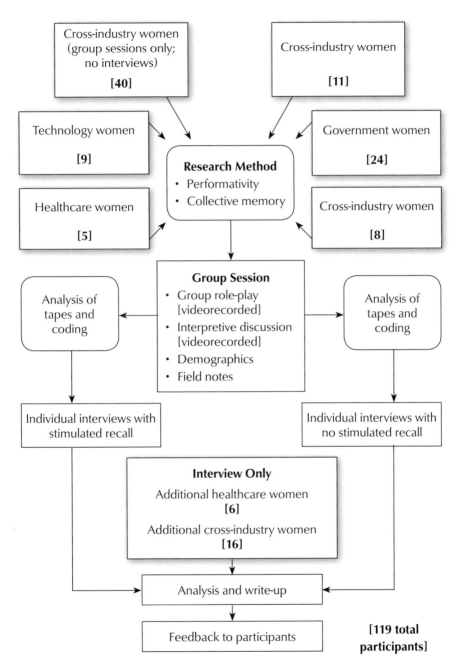

Figure 2. Research design—a feminist ethnographic study of patterns of relationship between women in the workplace

consent form before the session began. Some participants worked for the same organization, but recruitment criteria specified that intact work groups would not be eligible to participate. Only women were eligible to participate in the study. Study participants received a written summary of the study results if they chose this option.

Notes

Preface

1.   Lyn Mikel Brown, *Girlfighting: Betrayal and Rejection among Girls* (New York: New York University Press, 2003); Rosabeth M. Kanter, *Men and Women of the Corporation* (New York: Basic Books, 1977); Dan Kindlon and Michael Thompson, *Raising Cain: Protecting the Emotional Life of Boys* (New York: Ballantine Books, 1999); Rachel Simmons, *Odd Girl Out: The Hidden Culture of Aggression in Girls* (New York: Harcourt, 2002); and Julia T. Wood, *Gendered Lives: Communication, Gender, and Culture*, 5th ed. (Belmont, CA: Wadsworth/Thompson Learning, 2003).

2.   For example, see the website for a nonprofit entitled Hardy Girls Healthy Women at http://www.hghw.org.

3.   Hanna Rosin, "The End of Men," *Atlantic,* July/August 2010; and US Bureau of Labor Statistics, Report 1040, February 2013, "Women in the Labor Force: A Databook" at http://www.bls.gov/cps/wlf-databook-2012.pdf.

4.   Rosin, "The End of Men"; and Carl Bialik, "Not All Differences in Earnings Are Created Equal," *Wall Street Journal*, April 10, 2010.

5.   Georges Desvaux, Sandrine Devillard-Hoellinger, and Mary C. Meaney, "A Business Case for Women," *McKinsey Quarterly,* September 2008.

Introduction

1.   Arlie Hochschild and Anne Machung, *The Second Shift: Working Families and the Revolution at Home* (London: Penguin Books, 2012).

2.   Terri Apter and Ruthellen Josselson, *Best Friends: The Pleasures and Perils of Girls' and Women's Friendships* (New York: Crown, 1998); and Luise Eichenbaum and Susie Orbach, *Between Women: Love, Envy, and Competition in Women's Friendships* (New York: Viking Press, 1989), 10.

3.   Joyce K. Fletcher, *Disappearing Acts: Gender, Power and Relational Practice at Work* (Cambridge, MA: MIT Press, 1999); Judith V. Jordan, *Relational-Cultural Therapy* (Washington, DC: American Psychological Association, 2010); and Jean Baker Miller and Irene Pierce Stiver, *The Healing Connection: How Women Form Relationships in Therapy and in Life* (Boston: Beacon Press, 1997).

4.   Jordan, *Relational-Cultural Therapy*.

5.   Judith Briles, *Woman to Woman 2000: Becoming Sabotage Savvy in the New Millennium* (Far Hills, NJ: New Horizon Press, 1999); Phyllis Chesler, *Woman's Inhumanity to Woman* (New York: Nation Books, 2001); and Leora Tannenbaum, *Catfight: Women and Competition* (New York: Seven Stories Press, 2002).

Chapter One

1.   Jordan, *Relational-Cultural Therapy*, 26. What I am calling "friendship rules" are the same as what Jordan, citing Miller and Stiver, *The Healing Connection*, called "relational images." Relational images are inner constructions and expectations we create out of our experiences and relationships. They develop early in life and are carried from one relationship to another, sometimes subject to modification (growth) and sometimes limiting our expectations in ways that anchor us in the relational past.

2.   See Brown, *Girlfighting*; and Simmons, *Odd Girl Out*.

3.   Sandra L. Bem, *The Lenses of Gender* (Princeton: Yale University Press, 1994); Julia T. Wood, ed., *Gendered Relationships* (London: Sage, 1996); and Wood, *Gendered Lives.*

4.   Apter and Josselson, *Best Friends*; Eichenbaum and Orbach, *Between Women*; Pat O'Connor, *Friendship between Women: A Critical Review* (New York: Guilford Press, 1992); and Lillian B. Rubin, *Just Friends: The Role of Friendship in Our Lives* (New York: Harper & Row, 1985).

5.   Anne H. Litwin and Lynn O'Brien Hallstein, "Shadows and Silences: How Women's Positioning and Unspoken Friendship Rules in Organizational Settings Cultivate Difficulties among Some Women at Work," *Women's Studies in Communication* 30, no. 1 (2007): 111–142; and Anne H. Litwin, "Women Working Together: Understanding Women's Relationships at Work," *CGO Insights,* Briefing Note No. 33 (March 2011).

6.   Kanter, *Men and Women of the Corporation.*

7.   Fletcher, *Disappearing Acts.*

8.   Table adapted by Anne Litwin and Tom Finn, based on Joyce K. Fletcher, "Relational Theory in the Workplace" in *The Complexity of Connection: Writings from the Stone Center's Jean Baker Miller Training Institute,* ed. Judith V. Jordan, Maureen Walker, and Linda M. Hartling (New York: Guildford Press, 2004), 270–298.

9.   See Brown, *Girlfighting*; and Simmons, *Odd Girl Out.*

10. Joyce K. Fletcher, Judith V. Jordan, and Jean Baker Miller, "Women and the Workplace: Applications of a Psychodynamic Theory," *American Journal of Psychodynamics* 60, no. 3 (2000): 256.

11. Daniel Goleman, *Emotional Intelligence: Why It Can Matter More Than IQ* (New York: Bantam, 1995).

12. Pat Heim and Susan Murphy with Susan K. Golant, *In the Company of Women: Indirect Aggression among Women: Why We Hurt Each Other and How to Stop* (New York: Penguin Putnam, 2001).

13. Jordan, *Relational-Cultural Therapy.*

Chapter Two

1. "Most Women Prefer Working for Men," *Telegraph*, August 13, 2009, http://www.telegraph.co.uk/news/uknews/6020123/most -women-prefer-working-for-men.html.

2. Goleman, *Emotional Intelligence*.

3. The Power Dead-Even Rule correlates to the flat-structure value described in table 2 as a feminine workplace value. Heim and Murphy, *In the Company of Women*.

4. Heim and Murphy, *In the Company of Women*, 53.

5. Patrice M. Buzzanell, "Reframing the Glass Ceiling as a Socially Constructed Process: Implications for Understanding and Change," *Communications Monographs* 62 (1995): 327–354; and Michaela D. E. Meyers, "Women Speak(ing): Forty Years of Feminist Contributions to Rhetoric and an Agenda for Feminist Rhetorical Studies," *Communication Quarterly* 55, no. 1 (2007): 1–17.

6. Sheryl Sandberg, *Lean In: Women, Work, and the Will to Lead* (New York: Knopf, 2013).

7. Sandberg, *Lean In*, cites research by Columbia University professor Frank Flynn and New York University professor Cameron Anderson conducted in 2003.

8. Sandberg, *Lean In*, 39.

9. Sandberg, *Lean In*.

10. Ibid.

11. Linda Babcock and Sara Laschever, *Women Don't Ask: The High Cost of Avoiding Negotiation—and Positive Strategies for Change* (New York: Bantam, 2007); and Linda Babcock and Sara Laschever, *Ask for It: How Women Can Use the Power of Negotiation to Get What They Really Want* (New York: Bantam, 2008).

12. Heather Foust-Cummings, Sarah Dinolfo, and Jennifer Kohler, "Sponsoring Women to Success," *Catalyst Monograph* (2011); Hermina Ibarra, Nancy M. Carter, and Christine Silva, "Why Men Still Get More Promotions Than Women," *Harvard Business Review* (September 2010): 8–85; Rosin, "The End of Men"; and Jennifer T. Nozawa, "The Glass Ceiling of Nonprofits: A Review of Gender

Inequality in US Nonprofit Organization Executives," Center for Public Policy and Administration, University of Utah, July 28, 2010, http://www.cppa.utah.edu/_documents/publications/nonprofit/the-glass-ceilingof-nonprofits.pdf.

13. Catalyst, "2012 Catalyst Census: Fortune 500 Women Executive Officers and Top Earners," December 11, 2012, http://www.catalyst.org/knowledge/2012-catalyst-census-fortune-500-women-executive-officers-and-top-earners.

14. Sandberg, *Lean In.*

15. Shantel's mind-set may reflect what Dennis Mumby describes as an organizational narrative that articulates organizational reality as "the natural order of things." Dennis K. Mumby, "The Political Function of Narrative in Organizations," *Communication Monographs* 54, no. 2 (1987): 113–127.

16. Jordan, *Relational-Cultural Therapy.*

17. Maureen Walker, "How Relationships Heal" in *How Connections Heal: Stories from Relational-Cultural Therapy,* ed. Maureen Walker and Wendy B. Rosen (New York: Guildford Press, 2004), 1–21.

18. Karen L. Ashcraft and Dennis K. Mumby, *Reworking Gender: A Feminist Communicology of Organizations* (Thousand Oaks, CA: Sage, 2004). Ashcraft and Mumby describe this as a gendered function of bureaucracy to discourage relationships because they are threatening to the status quo.

19. Fletcher, "Relational Theory in the Workplace."

20. Ibid.

21. Andrew Ross Sorkin, "Women in a Man's World," *New York Times*, April 3, 2013.

22. Sorkin, "Women in a Man's World."

23. Foust-Cummings, Dinolfo, and Kohler, "Sponsoring Women to Success"; Ibarra, Carter, and Silva, "Why Men Still Get More Promotions than Women"; and Catalyst, "2012 Catalyst Census."

Chapter Three

1. Patrice M. Buzzanell, "Gaining Voice: Feminist Organizational Communication Theorizing," *Management Communication Quarterly* 7 (1994): 339–383.

2. Miller and Stiver, *The Healing Connection*.

3. Jordan, *Relational-Cultural Therapy*, 1.

4. Jordan, *Relational-Cultural Therapy*; and Fletcher, Jordan and Miller, "Women and the Workplace."

5. Jordan, *Relational-Cultural Therapy*, cites Miller and Stiver, *The Healing Connection*.

6. Geert Hofstede and Gert Jan Hofstede, *Cultures and Organizations: Software of the Mind* (New York: McGraw-Hill, 2005).

7. Alison Andrew and Jane Montague, "Women's Friendships at Work," *Women's Studies International Forum* 21, no. 4 (1998): 355–361. This article describes the work of Janice G. Raymond on the need for women to exercise "discernment" in forming friendships at work in her book, *A Passion for Friends: Toward a Philosophy of Female Affection* (Boston: Beacon Press, 1986).

8. Marsha Houston and Karla D. Scott, "Negotiating Boundaries, Crossing Borders" in *The Sage Handbook of Gender and Communication,* ed. Bonnie J. Dow and Julia T. Wood (Thousand Oaks, CA: Sage, 2006): 397–414.

Chapter Four

1. Buzzanell, "Gaining Voice" cites the work of Deborah M. Kolb, "Women's Work: Peacemaking in Organizations" in *Hidden Conflict in Organizations: Uncovering Behind the Scenes Disparities,* ed. Deborah M. Kolb and Jean M. Bartunek (Thousand Oaks, CA: Sage, 1992): 63–91. Kolb's work suggests that a number of indirect behavior patterns often associated with women, such as gossip, triangulated communication, and conflicted avoidance can be understood as relational behaviors evolving from concern about maintaining community.

2.   Kanter, *Men and Women of the Corporation*; and Miller and Stiver, *The Healing Connection*.

3.   Deborah Tannen, *Gender and Discourse* (Oxford: Oxford University Press, 1994).

4.   Edward T. Hall, *Understanding Cultural Differences* (Yarmouth, ME: Intercultural Press, 1990).

5.   Ella L. J. Edmonston Bell and Stella M. Nkomo, *Our Separate Ways: Black and White Women and the Struggle for Professional Identity* (Boston: Harvard University Press, 2001); and Marsha Houston, "Multiple Perspectives: African American Women Conceive Their Talk," *Women and Language* 23, no. 1 (2000): 11–18.

6.   Bell and Nkomo, *Our Separate Ways*.

7.   Patricia H. Collins, *Black Feminist Thought: Knowledge, Consciousness, and the Politics of Empowerment* (New York: Routledge, 1990), 217.

8.   Wood, *Gendered Relationships*.

9.   Jordan, *Relational-Cultural Therapy*.

10.   Miller and Stiver, *The Healing Connection*.

11.   Jordan, *Relational-Cultural Therapy*.

12.   Ibid.

13.   Ibid., 25.

Chapter Five

1.   Peggy Drexler, "The Tyranny of the Queen Bee," *Wall Street Journal*, March 2–3, 2013.

2.   Pauline R. Clance and Suzanne Imes, "The Imposter Phenomenon in High-Achieving Women: Dynamics and Therapeutic Intervention," *Psychotherapy: Theory, Research, and Practice* 15, no. 3 (Fall 1978).

3.   Paolo Freire, *Pedagogy of the Oppressed* (New York: Continuum, 1970), 62.

4.   Elizabeth Janeway, *Powers of the Weak* (New York: Knopf, 1980).

5.   Drexler, "Tyranny of the Queen Bee."

6. Brown, *Girlfighting*; and Simmons, *Odd Girl Out*.

7. Ibid.

8. Michael G. Thompson, Lawrence J. Cohen, and Catherine O'Neil Grace, *Best Friends, Worst Enemies: Understanding the Social Lives of Children* (New York: Ballantine, 2001).

9. Simmons, *Odd Girl Out*, 18.

10. Freire, *Pedagogy of the Oppressed*.

11. Lyn Mikel Brown and Carol Gilligan, *Meeting at the Crossroads: Women's Psychology and Girls' Development* (Cambridge, MA: Harvard University Press, 1992); and Brown, *Girlfighting*.

12. Simmons, *Odd Girl Out*.

13. Ibid.

14. Ibid.

15. Lyn Mikel Brown, *Raising Their Voices: The Politics of Girls' Anger* (Cambridge, MA: Harvard University Press, 1998); Peggy Orenstein, *School Girls: Young Women, Self-Esteem, and the Confidence Gap* (New York: Doubleday, 1994); Simmons, *Odd Girl Out*; and Virginia Valien, *Why So Slow? The Advancement of Women* (Cambridge, MA: MIT Press, 1998).

16. Brown, *Girlfighting*; and Simmons, *Odd Girl Out*.

17. Brown, *Raising Their Voices*.

18. Apter and Josselson, *Best Friends*.

19. Drexler, "Tyranny of the Queen Bee."

20. Simmons, *Odd Girl Out*.

21. Ibid., 47.

22. Ibid., 46.

23. Brown, *Girlfighting*; and Simmons, *Odd Girl Out*.

24. Briles, *Woman to Woman 2000*.

25. Jordan, *Relational-Cultural Therapy*.

26. Ibid.

Chapter Six

1. Jordan, *Relational-Cultural Therapy*.

2. Ibid., 4.

3.   Lee Gardenswartz and Anita Rowe, *Managing Diversity: A Complete Desk Reference and Planning Guide* (New York: Irwin, 1993).

4.   This model was developed by Alexandra Merrill and Joyce Weir, pioneers in women's leadership development training.

5.   Rita Andrews and Rosemary Bova, "Women to Women…A New Lens for Understanding Female Relationships" (unpublished monograph, 2001).

6.   Kim Lee DeAngelis, Senior HR Consultant, personal communication, August 6, 2013.

Chapter Seven

1.   Evangelina Holvino, "Time, Space and Social Justice in the Age of Globalization: Research and Applications on the Simultaneity of Differences," *Practising Social Change* 5 (May 2012).

2.   Mieke Verloo, "Intersectionality: From Theory to Policy and Practice" (presentation, Intersectionality: What's Missing and What's Not? Simmons College, Boston, MA, June 29–July 1, 2013). Verloo presented the concept of Gender Plus in her presentation, stating that gender never stands alone but can be understood only as it interacts with other dimensions of difference.

3.   Holvino, "Time, Space and Social Justice."

4.   Another difference that we need to be aware of is the continuum of gender identity—which tells us that many people do not identify as either a man or a woman, but as somewhere on a continuum. Another set of barriers is raised for these people in organizations when coworkers become uncomfortable with not being able to fit them into the binary box of female or male.

5.   Holvino, "Time, Space and Social Justice."

6.   A Nuyorican is a person born in New York of Puerto Rican parents.

7.   Jonathan Weisman and Jennifer Steinhauer, "Senate Women Lead in Effort to Find Accord," *New York Times*, October 15, 2013.

8.   Bell and Nkomo, *Our Separate Ways.*

9.   Janeway, *Powers of the Weak.*

10. Lynn O'Brien Hallstein, "Where Standpoint Stands Now: An Introduction and Commentary," *Women's Studies in Communication* 23, no. 1 (2000): 1–15.

11. Uma Narayan and Sandra Harding, eds., *Decentering the Center: Philosophy for a Multicultural, Postcolonial, and Feminist World* (Bloomington: Indiana University Press, 2000); and Verloo, "Intersectionality." As discussed by Verloo in her presentation, "zooming in and zooming out" describes a practice for holding both the general and the specific in the study of gender as it intersects with other differences.

12. Bell and Nkomo, *Our Separate Ways*; Brown, *Girlfighting*; and Collins, *Black Feminist Thought*.

13. Brown, *Girlfighting*.

14. Bell and Nkomo, *Our Separate Ways*.

15. Holvino, "Time, Space and Social Justice."

16. Sophia Kerby, "How Pay Inequity Hurts Women of Color," Center for American Progress, April 9, 2013, http://www .americanprogress.org/issues/labor/report/2013/04/09/59731/how -pay-inequity-hurts-women-of-color/; and "Closing the Wage Gap Is Crucial for Women of Color and Their Families," National Women's Law Center, April, 2013, http://www.nwlc.org/resource/closing-wage -gap-crucial-women-color-and-their-families.

17. Christianne Corbett and Catherine Hill, *Graduating to a Pay Gap: The Earnings of Women and Men One Year after College Graduation* (Washington, DC: American Association of University Women, 2012), http://www.aauw.org/research/graduating-to-a-pay-gap.

18. Tom Finn, *Are You Clueless? 7 Clues to Profit, Productivity & Partnership for Leaders in a Multicultural World* (Reston, VA: Kells Castle Press, 2007).

19. Bell and Nkomo, *Our Separate Ways*; Aida Hurtado, "Relating to Privilege: Seduction and Rejection in the Subordination of White Women and Women of Color," *Signs* 14, no. 4, (2000): 833–855; and Aida Hurtado, *The Color of Privilege* (Ann Arbor: University of Michigan Press, 1996).

20. Charles W. Mills, *The Racial Contract* (Ithaca, NY: Cornell University Press, 1997), 25–29.

21. Mills, *Racial Contract*, 13.

22. Amina Mama, *Beyond the Masks: Race, Gender and Subjectivity* (London: Routledge, 1995), 102.

23. Verloo, "Intersectionality."

Chapter Eight

1. William G. Dyer, W. Gibb Dyer, Jr., and Jeffrey H. Dyer, *Team Building: Proven Strategies for Improving Team Performance*, 4th ed. (San Francisco: Jossey-Bass, 2007).

Appendix

1. Leonard Bickman and Debra J. Rog, eds., *Handbook of Applied Social Research Methods* (Thousand Oaks, CA: Sage, 1998).

2. David M. Fetterman, "Ethnography," in *Handbook of Applied Social Research Methods*, ed. Leonard Bickman and Debra J. Rog (Thousand Oaks, CA: Sage, 1998), 495.

3. Shulamit Reinharz, *Feminist Methods in Social Research* (Oxford: Oxford University Press, 1992).

4. Ibid., 46.

5. Ibid., 71.

6. Erving Goffman, *The Presentation of Self in Everyday Life* (New York: Anchor Books, 1959).

7. Apter and Josselson, *Best Friends*; O'Connor, *Friendship between Women*; and Rubin, *Just Friends*.

8. O'Connor, *Friendship between Women*, 192.

9. Frigga Haug, *Female Sexualization: A Collective Work of Memory* (London: Verso, 1987), 60.

10. Ibid., 41.

11. Ibid., 60.

12. Goffman, *The Presentation of Self*, 35.

13. Debbie S. Dougherty and Kathleen J. Krone, "Overcoming the Dichotomy: Cultivating Standpoints in Organizations through Research," *Women's Studies in Communication* 23, no. 1 (2000): 25.

14. Goffman, *The Presentation of Self*, 73.

15. Ibid., 35.

16. Ibid., 80.

17. Dorinne K. Kondo, *About Face: Performing Race in Fashion and Theater* (New York, Routledge, 1997), 20.

18. Maurice Halbwachs, *The Collective Memory* (New York: Harper Colophon, 1980); Maurice Halbwachs, *On Collective Memory* (Chicago: University of Chicago Press, 1992); Haug, *Female Sexualization*; Jeffrey K. Olick and Joyce Robbins, "Social Memory Studies: From 'Collective Memory' to the Historical Sociology of Mnemonic Practices," *Annual Review of Sociology* 24 (1998): 104–140; and Barry Schwartz, "The Social Context of Commemoration: A Study of Collective Memory," *Social Forces* 61, no. 2 (1982): 374–402.

19. Haug, *Female Sexualization*, 42.

20. Ibid., 44.

21. Halbwachs, *The Collective Memory*, 22.

22. Haug, *Female Sexualization*, 46; Halbwachs, *The Collective Memory*, 24.

23. Haug, *Female Sexualization*, 56.

24. Susan M. Gass and Alison Mackey, *Stimulated Recall Methodology in Second Language Research* (Hillsdale, NJ: Lawrence Erlbaum Associates, 2000).

25. Carol A. B. Warren and Tracy X. Karner, *Discovering Qualitative Methods: Field Research, Interviews, and Analysis* (Los Angeles: Roxbury, 2005).

Index

The letter *t* following a page number denotes a table.

Anne H. Litwin, PhD
Consultant, Coach, Trainer, and Author

D r. Anne Litwin has been a consultant, coach, and trainer for more than thirty years in a wide variety of organizations throughout the world, including in North America, Asia, Europe, and Africa. She served as the CEO of her family business and was past chair of the board of directors and current professional member of the National Training Laboratories Institute. The findings from Anne's lifelong interest in the unique dynamics among women in a wide range of work environments is at the forefront of unlocking myths about women's work relationships.

Anne specializes in helping organizations leverage diversity, including gender differences, for business success. She has designed and facilitated workshops on women's leadership development and women and men working together, as well as change management processes to help organizations create more inclusive cultures. She also provides executive coaching to help executives, managers, and other professionals enhance their leadership capacity. She works with clients to improve their ability to communicate their ideas, to listen, to give and receive feedback, to manage conflict, and to deal effectively with system power dynamics. Anne helps her clients understand how to take diversity and international regional differences into account as managers, with colleagues, and with customers. Her clients range from small nonprofits to Fortune 100 companies and have included Aera Energy, Alibaba, Chevron, Siemens,

Hewlett-Packard, Microsoft, Texas Instruments, Hasbro, Parsons, Lucent Technologies, Verizon, Agilent, Novartis, Alcon, Pfizer Pharmaceuticals, Community Catalyst, and the Union of Concerned Scientists.

She has a bachelor's degree from the University of Wisconsin, a master's in community psychology from Marist College, and a master's and doctorate in human and organizational systems from Fielding Graduate University. She is a qualified user of the Myers-Briggs Type Indicator and the Leadership Circle Profile, a certified Organization Workshop trainer, a Future Search and World Café facilitator, and a member of the Organization Development Network. She is a coeditor of the book *Managing in the Age of Change*, as well as a coauthor of numerous articles on gender differences, women's leadership, and organization development consulting in the global context.

Anne lives in Boston, Massachusetts, with her life partner, Michael Willard. She can be contacted at info@annelitwin.com.

About Anne Litwin and Associates

Anne Litwin and Associates (ALA) provides leadership, team, and organization consulting services. ALA specializes in unleashing the leadership potential of women in organizations and helping organizations keep talented women and groom them as future leaders.

One key to increasing retention of talented women is to strengthen the ability of both female and male managers to create supportive environments where female staff can flourish. ALA helps organizations and leaders create these environments through a variety of proven processes and programs that include the following:

- **Keynote presentations** include topics such as understanding gender differences in the workplace, understanding women's relationships in the workplace, and other related subjects.

- **Women's leadership retreats** are designed to increase awareness of gender differences, the gendered workplace, and double binds for women bosses and to create a shared vision of women supporting each other at work.

- **Workshops for women and men** teach attendees about women and men in the workplace, skills development for overcoming conflicts based on gender socialization, effective interpersonal communication, managing role boundaries, and negotiating relationship expectations between women at work.

- **Executive coaching** is designed to provide individual leadership development.

- **Consulting services** are offered to help leaders plan and manage culture change initiatives to create inclusive work environments.

For more information about our services, contact ALA at info@ annelitwin.com.